ALIVE IN CHRIST

GRADE 1

Jesus Christ

aliveinchrist.osv.com

Our Sunday Visitor

The Subcommittee on the Catechism, United States Conference of Catholic Bishops, has found this catechetical series, copyright 2014, to be in conformity with the *Catechism of the Catholic Church*.

Nihil Obstat
Rev. Fr. Jeremiah L. Payne, S.Th.L.
Censor Librorum, Diocese of Orlando

Imprimatur
✠ Most Rev. John Noonan
Bishop of Orlando
March 26, 2013

Write:
Our Sunday Visitor Curriculum Division
Our Sunday Visitor, Inc.
200 Noll Plaza, Huntington, Indiana 46750

Alive in Christ is a registered trademark of Our Sunday Visitor Curriculum Division, Our Sunday Visitor, 200 Noll Plaza, Huntington, Indiana 46750.

For permission to reprint copyrighted materials, grateful acknowledgment is made to the following sources:

Excerpts from the English translation of *Rite of Baptism for Children* © 1969, International Commission on English in the Liturgy Corporation (ICEL); excerpts from the English translation of *The Liturgy of the Hours* © 1973, 1974, 1975, ICEL; excerpts from the English translation of Rite of Penance © 1974, ICEL; excerpts from the English translation of *The Roman Missal* © 2010, ICEL. All rights reserved.

Scripture selections taken from the *New American Bible, revised edition* © 2010, 1991, 1986, 1970 by the Confraternity of Christian Doctrine, Washington, D.C., and are used by license of the copyright owner. All rights reserved. No part of the *New American Bible* may be reproduced in any form without permission in writing from the copyright owner.

Excerpts from the *United States Catholic Catechism for Adults*, copyright © 2006, United States Catholic Conference, Inc.—Libreria Editrice Vaticana.

Music selections copyright John Burland, used with permission, and produced in partnership with Ovation Music Services, P.O. Box 402 Earlwood NSW 2206, Australia. Please refer to songs for specific copyright dates and information.

Music selections copyrighted or administered by OCP Publications are used with permission of OCP Publications, 5536 NE Hassalo, Portland, OR 97213. Please refer to songs for specific copyright dates and information.

Allelu! Growing and Celebrating with Jesus ® *Music CD* © Our Sunday Visitor, Inc. Music written and produced by Sweetwater Productions. All rights of the owners of these works are reserved.

Additional acknowledgments appear on page 389.

Alive in Christ School Grade 1 Student Book
ISBN: 978-1-61278-007-8
Item Number: CU5097

2 3 4 5 6 7 8 9 015016 21 20 19 18 17
Webcrafters, Inc., Madison, WI, USA; May 2017; Job# 130997

Contents at a Glance

Contents in Detail

UNIT 4: The Church

© Our Sunday Visitor

Catholic Social Teaching Live Your Faith . . . 342

*These pages introduce you to important teachings of Jesus and the
Church that help us live Jesus' New Commandment to love as he loved.*

Our Catholic Tradition Faith Basics 356

*This reference section presents information on our Creeds,
Sacraments, morality, prayers, and practices of our Catholic faith.*

Catholic Faith Words 383

Index 386

A New Year

 **Let Us Pray**

Leader: We shout joyfully to you, God.

"Know that the LORD is God,
he made us, we belong to him,
we are his people, the flock he
shepherds." Psalm 100:3

All: Thank you, God, for guiding and loving us.
Amen.

God's Word

"Thomas said to him, 'Master, we do not know
where you are going; how can we know the way?'

Jesus said to him, 'I am the way and the
truth and the life. No one comes to the Father
except through me. If you know me, then you
will also know my Father. From now on you do
know him and have seen him.'" John 14:5–7

What Do You Wonder?

- What does it mean to be
  a child of God?

- How does God invite us to
  know and love him?

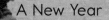

First Grade

What's the year going to be like?

This year you will learn many new things about our Catholic faith. You will learn about God's love for you. You will grow as Jesus' friend.

🔲 means the story or reading is from the Bible. Through Bible stories you will meet Jesus.

♥ lets you know it's time to pray. You will grow closer to Jesus as you pray and get to know his teachings.

▶ tells you to sing songs to praise God and celebrate our faith.

> **Underline one thing you will do this year.**

The gold star above begins an exercise to help you learn what's being taught. You may underline, circle, write, match, or draw.

In every chapter you will see a link to the Our Catholic Tradition section of your book. This link will lead you to more information about topics of your Catholic faith.

2

Ways to Know God

During this year, you'll discover how we are made by God. He gives us the gifts of his creation. You can know God through his Son, Jesus, and the Bible.

Jesus is the **Son of God** who loves you and shows you how to love the Father and one another.

We also know God through our families and the Church. Jesus is with his Church always, and the Holy Spirit is always guiding and helping us.

Catholic Faith Words

In this box you will see the highlighted words and their definitions.

Son of God a name for Jesus that tells you God is his Father. The Son of God is the Second Divine Person of the Holy Trinity.

Activity

When you see these fun green words, you know it's time for an activity!

Think Who is the Son of God? Color in his name.

Share Share your work with a classmate.

God's Word

What can we learn from the Bible?

The **Bible** is the Word of God.

The Bible has two parts. The first part is the Old Testament. It is about the times before Jesus was born. The second part is the New Testament. It tells about Jesus and his followers.

In the Bible there are many kinds of stories. From these stories we learn about God and his love. We hear about how God wants us to live.

© Our Sunday Visitor

Catholic Faith Words

Bible the Word of God written in human words. The Bible is the holy book of the Church.

From the Old Testament — God's Creation

From the New Testament — The Nativity

The Gospels

Some of the most important Bible stories are about Jesus. We find these stories in the Gospels, the first four books of the New Testament.

We learn about Jesus' birth and life. We hear stories Jesus used to help us understand he is the Son of God who leads us to God the Father.

Activity

Draw a Bible Story
Draw your favorite story from the Bible.

Our Catholic Life

What does it mean to be Catholic?

Each chapter in your book has an Our Catholic Life section with activities that help us grow closer to Jesus and the Church.

Grow as a Follower of Jesus

- know more about our faith
- learn about the Sacraments
- live as Jesus calls us to
- talk and listen to God in prayer
- take part in Church life
- help others know about Jesus

People of Faith

Look for this box, where you will meet People of Faith, holy women and men who loved God very much and did his work on Earth.

Activity

Friend of Jesus You are a friend of Jesus. Write your name.

Audrey Wallach

Pray Together

Every chapter has a prayer. You may ask God for help, thank him, pray for others, and praise him with songs.

Gather and begin with the Sign of the Cross.

All: In the name of the Father, and of the Son, and of the Holy Spirit. Amen.

Leader: Let us pray.

Bow your heads as the leader prays.

All: Amen.

Leader: A reading from the holy Gospel according to John.

Read John 6:12.

The Gospel of the Lord.

All: Praise to you, Lord Jesus Christ.

 Sing "Alive in Christ"

We are Alive in Christ
We are Alive in Christ
He came to set us free
We are Alive in Christ
We are Alive in Christ
He gave his life for me
We are Alive in Christ
We are Alive in Christ

FAMILY+FAITH
LIVING AND LEARNING TOGETHER

YOUR CHILD LEARNED >>>

This page is for you, the parent, to encourage you to talk about your faith and see the many ways you already live your faith in daily family life.

God's Word

 In this section, you will find a Scripture citation and a summary of what your child has learned in the chapter.

Catholics Believe

- Bulleted information highlights the main points of doctrine of the chapter.

People of Faith

Here you meet the holy person featured in People of Faith.

CHILDREN AT THIS AGE >>>

This feature gives you a sense of how your child, at this particular age, will likely understand what is being taught. It suggests ways you can help your child better understand, live, and love their faith.

How They Understand the Lessons Your first-grader is making an important transition from your family circle into the wider world. Making friends is important for them. It is common for them to feel intense but brief attachments. They may have a new best friend every few days. While they are still somewhat gracefully self-centered, they like helping others and need opportunities to do so.

Children this age think and learn concretely. When talking about God with your child, use concrete images and experiences.

Repetition and recognition work well with the first-grader. Say the same prayers together often. Determine what religious rituals will be consistently used in your home.

For most young children praying is as natural as talking and listening to a family member or friend. Encourage your child to spontaneously pray aloud at meals or when preparing to go to bed.

CONSIDER THIS >>>

This section includes a question that invites you to reflect on your own experience and consider how the Church speaks to you on your own faith journey.

LET'S TALK >>>

- Here you will find some practical questions that prompt discussion about the lesson's content, faith sharing, and making connections with your family life.

- Ask your child to name one thing they've learned about their book.

LET'S PRAY >>>

 This section encourages family prayer connected to the example of our People of Faith.

Holy men and women, pray for us. Amen.

 For a multimedia glossary of Catholic Faith Words, Sunday readings, seasonal and Saint resources, and chapter activities go to **aliveinchrist.osv.com**.

Mary's Birthday

 Let Us Pray

Leader: Dear Mother Mary,
Happy Birthday! Thank you for being
Jesus' Mother. Help us to be like him.

"Most blessed are you among women."
Luke 1:42

All: Amen.

God's Word

"My soul proclaims the greatness of the Lord; my spirit rejoices in God my savior. For he has looked upon his handmaid's lowliness; behold, from now on will all ages call me blessed. The Mighty One has done great things for me, and holy is his name." Luke 1:46-49

What Do You Wonder?

- How is Mary blessed?
- Why do we honor Mary?

Mother Mary

Why does the Church honor Mary?

You are God's child. Because God is your Father, Jesus is your Brother.

The Mother of Jesus is Mary. Mary is your mother, too. Mary said "yes" to God's plan for her, and the Son of God became man.

We celebrate Mary's birthday on September 8. The color for the feasts of Mary is white.

Ordinary Time

- Ordinary Time celebrates the words and works of Jesus.

- This season is marked by the color green.

- There are many feasts of Mary in this season.

Ordinary Time

Ordinary Time is a season of the Church year that comes twice, once after Christmas and for a longer time after Easter. During this time we learn more about Jesus' teachings so we can grow as his disciples. We also honor Mary and many of the Saints.

Our Catholic Tradition
For more, go to page **379**

Underline when Ordinary Time comes during the Church year.

➤ **Why do we honor Mary?**

Activity

Honor Mary You honor Mary when you say "yes" to God. Color in the picture of Mary and Jesus.

© Our Sunday Visitor

Say "Yes" to God Mary said "yes" to God! She trusted in God and said "yes" to his plan for her. Match the pictures below with the ways that you can say "yes" to God.

●   ● I can go to Mass.

●   ● I can be kind.

●   ● I can pray.

Share with a classmate about a time that someone in your family said "yes" to God.

Our Catholic Life

Good people are all around you. Who are some good people you know? How can you be more like them?

The Holy Spirit guides you to do good actions. **Goodness** is a Fruit of the Holy Spirit. Goodness grows in you every time you obey your parents. You practice goodness when you do acts of kindness for others. When you make choices to do good loving actions God's goodness grows in you.

During the Church year we celebrate Mary, the Mother of God. She shows us goodness. Every time she said "yes" to God, her goodness grew and grew. You can say, "yes", too.

Fruits of the Holy Spirit

The twelve **Fruits of the Holy Spirit** are what others can see in us when we let the Holy Spirit work in our hearts. This season we are focusing on **Goodness.**

Activity

A Garden of Goodness
Think of one good action you will do to grow goodness and color your garden.

13

People of Faith

Saint Patrick

Saint Rose of Lima

Saint Moses the Black

Chapter	Person	Feast Day
1	Blessed Fra Angelico	February 18
2	Saint Nicholas	December 6
3	Saint Albert the Great	November 15
4	Saint Patrick	March 17
5	Zechariah, Elizabeth & John	November 5 and June 24
6	Saint Paul of the Cross	October 20
7	Saint Louise de Marillac	March 15
8	Saint Thomas of Villanova	September 22
9	Saint Ephrem the Hymnist	June 9
10	Blessed Mary Theresa of the Child Jesus	May 9
11	Saint Rose of Lima	August 23
12	Saint Dominic	August 8
13	Venerable Father Solanus Casey	
14	Saint Frances Cabrini	November 13
15	Saint Dismas	March 25
16	Saint Giuseppina Bakhita	February 8
17	Mary	January 1
18	Saint Moses the Black	August 28
19	Pope Saint John XXIII	October 11
20	Saint Emily de Vialar	June 17
21	Saint Pedro Calungsod	April 2

 **Let Us Pray**

Ave Maria

Gather and begin by singing the refrain.

 Sing "Immaculate Mary"

Pray the Sign of the Cross together.

Leader: Blessed be God.

All: Blessed be God forever.

Bow your head as the leader prays.

All: Amen.

Listen to God's Word

Leader: A reading from the holy Gospel according to Matthew.

Read Matthew 1:18-23.

The Gospel of the Lord.

All: Praise to you, Lord Jesus Christ.

Leader: Let us go to share God's peace and love.

All: Thanks be to God.

FAMILY+FAITH
LIVING AND LEARNING TOGETHER

TALKING ABOUT ORDINARY TIME >>>

Feasts of Mary and the Saints occur all during the Church year. The celebration of Mary's birthday on September 8th comes in Ordinary Time. Ordinary Time is the longest of all the Church seasons. In celebrating Mary's birthday, the Church gives expression to her birth as a special moment in salvation history. She would give birth to Jesus, the Savior. She is the Mother of God. By celebrating Mary's birthday, we rejoice that she was open to God's invitation to become the Mother of Jesus.

God's Word

Read **Luke 1:46-56**, the Magnificat of Mary. It is one of the choices for the responsorial psalms sung or recited at a Mass honoring Mary.

HELPING YOUR CHILD UNDERSTAND >>>
Mary

- Most children this age have great affection for Mary as Jesus' Mother.

- At this age children should be familiar with the Hail Mary but need help with the words (see page 379).

- Your child will be able to identify with Mary's response of "yes" to what God asked of her.

CATHOLIC FAMILY CUSTOMS >>>

Mary's Birth One of the ways to celebrate the birth of Mary is to honor mothers you know. It is also a perfect time to talk about life as a gift. You can talk about why it is important to celebrate life at birthdays and why as Catholics we care for every form of life, including all of creation.

Talk about the many "mothers" who have helped you in your life. Include your own mother and grandmother as well as aunts, mothers of friends, and others.

Brainstorm what special thing each of you can do to honor one of the mothers you have talked about. Possibilities might be to bring her flowers, write a note, draw a picture for her, or pray for her.

© Our Sunday Visitor

FAMILY PRAYER >>>

Pray this prayer of trust in Mary together during the month of September.

Mary, Mother of Jesus and my Mother, too, help me to say "yes" to God every day. Amen.

For a multimedia glossary of Catholic Faith Words, Sunday readings, seasonal and Saint resources, and chapter activities go to **aliveinchrist.osv.com**.

All Saints Day

 Let Us Pray

Leader: Dear God, our Father, we are your children. We love you. We want to stay close to you always.

"I am the light of the world. Whoever follows me will not walk in darkness, but will have the light of life." John 8:12

All: Amen.

God's Word

"As the Father loves me, so I also love you. Remain in my love. If you keep my commandments, you will remain in my love.... I have told you this so that my joy may be in you and your joy may be complete."

John 15:9–11

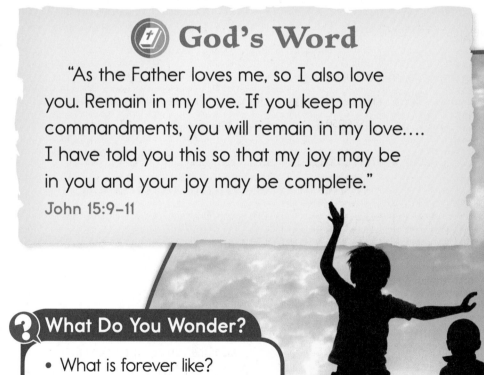

? What Do You Wonder?

- What is forever like?
- Who are the Saints?

Holy Lives

Why does the Church honor Saints?

All Saints Day is celebrated on November 1. It is a Holy Day of Obligation, which means that Catholics must attend Mass. The feast honors everyone who is in Heaven.

Circle the date that we honor all of the Saints in Heaven.

Our Catholic Tradition
For more, go to page 382

A Feast for Everyone

When people who love God very much and lead a holy life die, they go to Heaven to live forever with God. These heroes of the Church are called Saints. They are examples of how to live our faith.

We don't know the name of everyone in Heaven. On All Saints Day, Catholics also honor the Saints we can't name. On that day, we remember everyone in Heaven. We also honor Saints on feast days during the year.

In April, we celebrate the Feast of Saint Joseph.

Activity

Patron Saints On All Saints Day we honor the holy men and women of the Church. Saints are often patrons of certain jobs and objects. Choose one of the patron Saints from the list below and draw the symbol for that Saint.

Saint Francis: Animals   Saint Augustine: A Book and Pen

Saint Lucy: Eyes   Saint Nicholas of Myra: Children

Saint Florian: Firemen   Saint Jerome: A Lion

What would you like to be the patron Saint of?

finding.

Our Catholic Life

Fruits of the Holy Spirit

The twelve Fruits of the Holy Spirit are what others can see in us when we let the Holy Spirit work in our hearts. This season we are focusing on Faithfulness.

Sarah thanked Carly for being such a good friend. "Remember when my Dad lost his job? You cheered me up. You played games with me when I was sad. You were a faithful friend."

Faithfulness is keeping your promises to love God and others. You are faithful when you pray. You are faithful when you help others.

On All Saints Day, we celebrate all the people who were faithful to God and now live forever with him in Heaven.

We honor them for being faithful to the promises of their Baptism. We will be like them if we are keep our promises to others and do what God wants us to do.

Activity

I Am Faithful Check off the actions you can do to show faithfulness.

- ☑ Go to Mass on Sunday
- ☒ Be unkind to my friend
- ☑ Share my games
- ☑ Be on time
- ☒ Tell a lie
- ☑ Do what I'm supposed to do without the teacher calling on me

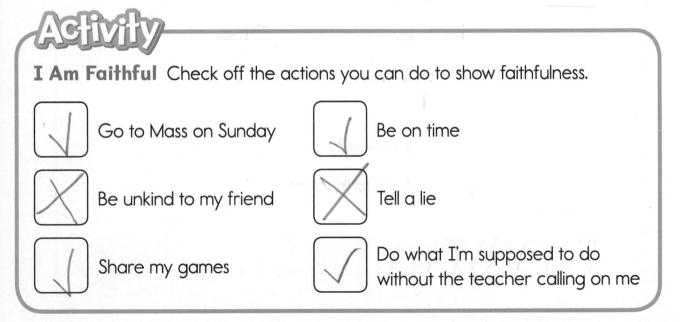

♥ Let Us Pray

Celebrate Holy Lives

Gather and begin with the Sign of the Cross.

Leader: Blessed be God.

All: Blessed be God forever.

Leader: Let us pray.

Bow your heads as the leader prays.

All: Amen.

Listen to God's Word

Leader: A reading from the holy Gospel according to John.

Read John 6:40.

The Gospel of the Lord.

All: Praise to you, Lord Jesus Christ.

Leader: Like the Saints, let us go out to serve the Lord.

All: Thanks be to God.

▶ Sing "Sing a Song to the Saints"

FAMILY+FAITH
LIVING AND LEARNING TOGETHER

TALKING ABOUT ORDINARY TIME >>>

On the Feast of All Saints we honor all the named and unnamed Saints. We honor the many people who are in Heaven, including those whom the Church has not officially canonized or named publicly as Saints. This feast reminds all of us that we are each called to be a Saint. For Catholics, this day is a Holy Day of Obligation.

God's Word

Read **John 15:9–17**, to learn how we are the branches who are attached to the Lord. It is from him that we receive the nourishment to love.

HELPING YOUR CHILD UNDERSTAND >>>

Saints

- Most children this age understand that Saints are friends of God.
- At this age, many children believe that good people they know who have died are in Heaven with God.
- In most cases children are motivated by the fact that they, too, can be Saints.

FEASTS OF THE SEASON >>>

Feast of All Saints
November 1

The Feast of All Saints is a great time to talk about your family's religious heritage. Tell your child family stories relating to religious celebrations. Talk about the people who most influenced your faith and who most revealed God to you, who taught you about God. God reveals himself to us in many ways, including creation, Scripture, Tradition, and people. To make the stories more concrete, share family pictures with your child. If you can do so comfortably, it is important to talk with your child about family members who have passed away and are in Heaven. Share the good things that they did, inspired by their faith.

FAMILY PRAYER >>>

 Say this prayer together at dinner on November 1 to celebrate the Feast of All Saints.

Dear God, you are the source of holiness. Everyone who is in Heaven honors you. Let us join our prayers with their prayers. And when we have finished our journey on Earth, bring us into their company. We ask this through Jesus, your Son. Amen.

For a multimedia glossary of Catholic Faith Words, Sunday readings, seasonal and Saint resources, and chapter activities go to **aliveinchrist.osv.com**.

Waiting for Jesus

 Let Us Pray

Leader: Lord Jesus, we are waiting for you. Show us what to do to get our hearts ready.

"To you, O LORD, I lift up my soul."
Psalm 25:1

All: Amen.

 God's Word

"The wilderness and the parched land will exult.... Like the crocus it shall bloom abundantly.... They will see the glory of the LORD, the splendor of our God." Isaiah 35:1–2

? What Do You Wonder?

- Why do we need to get ready for important events?
- How can we get ready for jesus?

Our Catholic Tradition

For more, go to page **367**

Circle the color that the priest wears during Advent.

Advent

- The season during the four weeks before Christmas.

- During this time we prepare to celebrate the coming of Jesus.

Get Ready

What is Advent?

Advent is the first season of the Church year. The priest wears purple colors in Advent. Purple is the color of royalty as we await the coming King. It is also the color for sorrow and feeling sorry.

People waited many years for God to send someone to save us. Finally, Jesus was born in Bethlehem.

Advent is a time to get our hearts ready for Jesus, our King, to return again in glory.

Activity

Getting Ready

What are some ways you get ready before going to school, going on a trip, or going to Mass?

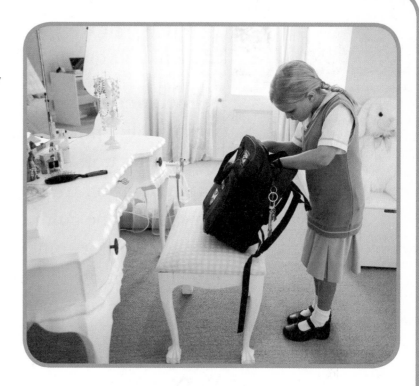

We can

pray

Advent is here. You have four weeks. What will you do to prepare for Jesus?

have a

advent-calender

Our Catholic Life

When you wait for something to happen, you are patient.

Patience is one of the twelve Fruits of the Holy Spirit. Patience helps you wait. When you are are waiting in line or taking turns on the computer, patience helps you to be calm and kind. When you pray to God for something and it doesn't happen right away, patience helps you wait for God's answer.

Advent is a time of waiting. During Advent we remember how patient the people were who waited for Jesus, the Savior, to come. We wait for his return at the end of time.

Fruits of the Holy Spirit

The twelve Fruits of the Holy Spirit are what others can see in us when we let the Holy Spirit work in our hearts. This season we are focusing on Patience.

Activity

My Patience Draw a picture of one way you will be patient during Advent.

26

 **Let Us Pray**

Prayer of Praise

Gather and begin with the Sign of the Cross.

Leader: Come, Lord Jesus.

All: Come, Lord Jesus.

Leader: Let us pray.

Bow your heads as the leader prays.

All: Amen.

Listen to God's Word

Leader: A reading from the holy Gospel according to Matthew.

Read Matthew 24:42.

The Gospel of the Lord.

All: Praise to you, Lord Jesus Christ.

 Sing "Stay Awake"

FAMILY+FAITH
LIVING AND LEARNING TOGETHER

TALKING ABOUT ADVENT >>>

Advent is the first season of the Church year. It is four weeks of preparing and waiting for the celebration of Christmas. The Church reminds us to take a step back during these weeks and recall the longings of those who waited for God to fulfill his promise of a Savior.

God's Word

 Read **Isaiah 35:1–6**, to learn how Isaiah gave the Israelites hope of God's promise to bring them home and to save them.

HELPING YOUR CHILD UNDERSTAND >>>
Advent

- Most children this age find waiting difficult. An Advent calendar is one way to help children get into the spirit of Advent waiting.

- Typically analogies help children this age understand what the season is about. To help your child get a sense of the season, use examples of waiting from their own experience, such as waiting for a special visitor.

- Sometimes the stimulation of preparing for Christmas can lead young children to excitability, whining, or other negative behaviors. Children (and adults) will respond well to quiet times of reflection and prayer using the psalms from the Sundays of Advent.

FEASTS OF THE SEASON >>>
Feast of Saint Nicholas
December 6

Legends abound about a bishop born in the third century who used his whole inheritance to assist the needy, the sick, and the suffering without wanting anything in return. Christmas gifts and seasonal contributions to charity reflect Saint Nicholas' unselfish concern for others. European immigrants brought these Christmas customs to America.

FAMILY PRAYER >>>

Say this prayer to bless your Advent wreath. Leader: Let us pray. O God, pour forth your blessing upon this wreath, and grant that we who use it may prepare our hearts for the coming of Christ and receive from you many blessings. (Sprinkle the wreath with Holy Water in the form of a cross. Have your child make the Sign of the Cross along with you.) Through Christ our Lord.
All: Amen.

For a multimedia glossary of Catholic Faith Words, Sunday readings, seasonal and Saint resources, and chapter activities go to **aliveinchrist.osv.com**.

The Light of Christ

 Let Us Pray

Leader: Dear Jesus,
Thank you for coming into the world.
Thank you for being our light.

"The people who walked in darkness
have seen a great light." Isaiah 9:1a

All: Amen.

🔲 God's Word

"The angel of the Lord appeared to them and the glory of the Lord shone around them, and… the angel said to them, 'Do not be afraid; for behold, I proclaim to you good news of great joy that will be for all the people. For today in the city of David a savior has been born for you who is Messiah and Lord.'" Luke 2:9–11

❓ What Do You Wonder?

- Why is light important?
- How is Jesus our Light?

A Season of Joy

How does the Church celebrate the Christmas season?

Our Catholic Tradition

For more, go to page 368

The Christmas season is more than one day. It is a season that lasts for a few weeks. It is a season of joy. The church is brightly decorated. The priest wears white or gold vestments. We see the Christmas Nativity scene in church for the whole season. During the season you hear about all the things that happened to Jesus as a young child.

Underline what you hear about during the Christmas season.

The Star of Bethlehem

The star of Bethlehem pointed the way to the Baby Jesus.

When you look at the star on your tree, think of the three wise men.

You will be wise, too, if you look for Jesus.

Are you a star?

One way you can be a star is to light the way to Jesus for others.

Who Brings the Light?

The star of Bethlehem showed the way to Jesus just like Jesus guides people and shows us the way to the Father. Trace the lines to make the star of Bethlehem. Then write the name of one person who brings Christ's light to you.

Audrey

The Star

Joceline

Jesus   Chloe

Our Catholic Life

Fruits of the Holy Spirit

The twelve **Fruits of the Holy Spirit** are what others can see in us when we let the Holy Spirit work in our hearts. This season we are focusing on **Generosity**

Li wanted to give his friend, Tom, a Christmas gift. Li decided to give Tom one of his toy trucks for Christmas. When he asked his mother, she said, "Li, that is very generous of you."

Generosity is one of the twelve Fruits of the Holy Spirit. Generosity helps us share what we have with others. God has been generous to you. God's generosity helps us to be generous. When you are generous, you are saying thank you to God.

The Christmas season is a season of generosity. We give and receive gifts. We celebrate Jesus, God's greatest gift to us.

Activity

Thank You God Finish the thank you note to God. Write the name of one of God's gifts you want to thank him for.

Dear God,

Thank you for your generous gift of _Love_

Love, _Life_

Audrey

 **Let Us Pray**

Celebrate Christmas

Gather and begin with the Sign of the Cross.

Leader: Blessed be the name of the Lord.

All: Now and forever.

Leader: Let us pray.

Bow your heads as the leader prays.

All: Amen.

Listen to God's Word

Leader: A reading from the holy Gospel according to Matthew.

Read Matthew 2:9–11.

The Gospel of the Lord.

All: Praise to you, Lord Jesus Christ.

Leader: Let us rejoice in the birth of Jesus.

All: Thanks be to God.

 Sing "Glory to God"

FAMILY+FAITH
LIVING AND LEARNING TOGETHER

TALKING ABOUT CHRISTMAS >>>

The Church celebrates the Christmas season beginning with the celebration of Christ's birth with a vigil on Christmas Eve, and ending with the celebration of the Baptism of the Lord in January. It is a festive season and includes several feasts commemorating the very early life of Jesus and the many ways God reveals himself to humans. White, the liturgical color for Christmas, is a symbol of new life. In the liturgies of the Church, the People of God celebrate with wonder, the Incarnation—God becomes flesh and dwells among us. We also celebrate that God the Father sent Jesus to save us.

God's Word

Read **Luke 2:1–14**. In the Gospel according to Luke there is a continual focus on Jesus reaching out to those who are on the margins of society, so it is not surprising that poor shepherds are the first to hear the Good News of Jesus' birth.

HELPING YOUR CHILD UNDERSTAND >>>
Christmas

- At this age most children identify with Christmas as the "birthday" of Jesus. It is helpful to deepen their awareness that we are also celebrating the fact that God came among us and still remains with us.

- Gift-getting is important at any age. Giving thanks for gifts is not always the first thing children think about at Christmas. Use this opportunity to help children find ways to express their gratitude for material and non-material gifts. They might also consider how many children do not receive Christmas gifts, and what they can do for those children.

CATHOLIC FAMILY CUSTOMS >>>
The Nativity Scene

Each time you thank a family member during this season or affirm one of their non-material gifts, you strengthen the awareness of God's presence in your family. Gather around the family Nativity scene. Ask the members of your family to extend their hands over the Nativity scene in a gesture of blessing. Say: "May our Christmas manger be a reminder that our hearts are a home for Jesus."

FAMILY PRAYER >>>

 Loving God, thank you for all the ways you share your love with us during this Christmas season. Show us how to live as generously as you do. Bless us and teach us to share with those in need. Amen.

For a multimedia glossary of Catholic Faith Words, Sunday readings, seasonal and Saint resources, and chapter activities go to **aliveinchrist.osv.com**.

Time for Change

 Let Us Pray

Leader: Lord, God, send your Holy Spirit to guide us to right and loving actions.

"Make known to me your ways, LORD; teach me your paths." Psalm 25:4

All: Amen.

God's Word

"Then God spoke all these words: I am the LORD your God, who brought you out of the land of Egypt, out of the house of slavery. You shall not have other gods beside me…. You shall not invoke the name of the LORD, your God, in vain…. Remember the sabbath day—keep it holy."
Exodus 20:1–3; 7–8

? What Do You Wonder?

- What can take us away from God?
- How can we put God first?

Lent

What do we celebrate during Lent?

Lent is a special time. It lasts forty days. The Church is getting ready for Easter!

Lent starts on Ash Wednesday. The ashes on your forehead remind you that Jesus came to save us.

The priest wears purple as a sign of our sorrow for the things that take us away from God.

© Our Sunday Visitor

Showing Love

Lent is a time when you pay special attention to putting God first. You put God first when you show love to God and others.

You can show love for God by listening to God's Word.

You can show love for God by praying at a special time every day.

Our Catholic Tradition

For more, go to page 378

You can show love for others by helping out at home.

You can show love for others by saying kind words to them.

➤ **What else can you do to show love during Lent?**

Draw one way you put God first during Lent.

© Our Sunday Visitor

Put God First

Jesus always put his Father first. We put God first in our lives when we show love in our words and actions.

Activity

How can you put God first? Draw a circle around the things you can do to put God first.

Activity

Signs of Lent During Lent, the color purple is used to remind us that we are preparing for Easter. Below are some others signs of Lent. Look at each of the signs and write what you think each one might mean.

Praying hands

The sign of the cross

A Heart for good

Our Catholic Life

Leah talks out of turn in class. Today her teacher asked the class a question. Several children raised their hands. Leah wanted to answer the question. She was about to call out the answer but she stopped. She put her hand up too. Leah practiced self-control.

Self-control is one of the Fruits of the Holy Spirit. Self-control is doing the right thing even when it's hard. The Holy Spirit guides you to do the right thing. When it's hard to do the right thing pray to the Holy Spirit to help you.

During the season of Lent we act to put God first. We practice self-control.

Fruits of the Holy Spirit

The twelve Fruits of the Holy Spirit are what others can see in us when we let the Holy Spirit work in our hearts. This season we are focusing on Self-Control

Activity

Right Action Chains
Think about right actions you can do during Lent.

As a class, make a list of right actions. Follow your teacher's directions and make a class right action chain.

 **Let Us Pray**

Celebrate Lent

Gather and begin with the Sign of the Cross.

Leader: Blessed be God.

All: Blessed be God forever.

Leader: Let us pray.

Bow your head as the leader prays.

All: Amen.

Listen to God's Word

Leader: A new heart, create for me, O God.
Give me a heart that loves only you.
Based on Psalm 51:12

All: A new heart, create for me, O God.
Give me a heart that loves only you.

Sing "God of Mercy"

God of mercy, you are with us.
Fill our hearts with your kindness.
God of patience, strong and gentle,
fill our hearts with your kindness.
Lord, have mercy. Lord, have mercy.
Lord, have mercy upon us.

FAMILY+FAITH

LIVING AND LEARNING TOGETHER

TALKING ABOUT LENT >>>

Lent is a forty day journey that begins on Ash Wednesday. The receiving of ashes on one's forehead marks one's promise to repent or change to grow closer to God and the Church. It includes the Lenten practices of fasting, prayer, and penance. During Lent the Church uses the color purple for Church vestments as a sign of repentance.

God's Word

 Read **Exodus 20:1–3; 7–8**, to hear God's command to put nothing else before him.

HELPING YOUR CHILD UNDERSTAND >>>

Lent

- At this age children can usually be drawn very easily into an understanding of Lent as a time to grow closer to God.
- Most children at this age will find that the music associated with Lent will draw them into the spirit of the season.
- Ordinarily at this age children are ready to learn that forgiveness and being sorry are more than just the words but need actions to follow.

FEASTS OF THE SEASON >>>

Saint Patrick's Day
March 17

Use a shamrock plant and talk with your child about how Saint Patrick used it to teach the Irish people about the Trinity. The three leaves of the shamrock plant remind us of the three Divine Persons in one God.

FAMILY PRAYER >>>

 Say this prayer together as a mealtime prayer during Lent.

Dear God, we thank you for all your gifts, for this food we are about to eat and for all of our family members. We know we have not always loved you or one another as you want us to. Help us to change and grow closer to you. Amen.

 For a multimedia glossary of Catholic Faith Words, Sunday readings, seasonal and Saint resources, and chapter activities go to **aliveinchrist.osv.com**.

Holy Week

 Let Us Pray

Leader: Dear Jesus, help us to grow in trust.
We pray this in your name.

"Blessed is he
who comes in the name of the LORD."
Psalm 118:26

All: Amen.

 **God's Word**

"Many people spread leafy branches that they had cut from the fields. They cried out Hosanna! Blessed is he who comes in the name of the Lord! Hosanna in the highest!" Based on Mark 11:8–10

? What Do You Wonder?

- Where was Jesus going when the people shouted Hosanna for him?
- What makes Holy Week so holy?

Time for Remembering

What special gift did Jesus give us?

On Palm Sunday, we remember how crowds welcomed Jesus into Jerusalem.

Jesus gave us a special gift. He gave his life for our sins. He died, but he was raised to new life. Palm Sunday marks the beginning of the holiest week of the year. We hear the words of the people to Jesus,

"Hosanna."   Matthew 21:9

During this Holy Week we remember Jesus' dying and rising in a special way, especially on these three holiest days:

• Holy Thursday

• Good Friday

• Holy Saturday

Our Catholic Tradition
For more, go to page **373**

 **Activity**

Unscramble the Word Unscramble the letters to find the word that we say when we celebrate on Palm Sunday.

NSAOHAN

Hosanna

Palm Sunday

Jesus came into the big city of Jerusalem.

His friends came with him.

Jesus rode on a donkey.

Many people stood along the road.

They put their cloaks on the ground in front of Jesus.

The people waved palm branches.

They shouted, "Hosanna in the highest."

We celebrate this day on Palm Sunday.

Activity

Draw a Palm Branch Draw yourself welcoming Jesus and waving a palm branch.

Our Catholic Life

Who loves you the most? Who are the people you love?

People show love in many ways. They share. They spend time with you. They give you a hug.

Charity (Love) is a Fruit of the Holy Spirit. Another name for love is charity. Charity guides you to love God the most, to love others and to love yourself. Charity grows in you when you do loving acts. The more you show love, the more you become like Jesus.

Holy Week celebrates Jesus' greatest gift of love to us. He loved us so much he gave up his own life for us. He died on the Cross for us so our sins would be forgiven.

Fruits of the Holy Spirit

The twelve Fruits of the Holy Spirit are what others can see in us when we let the Holy Spirit work in our hearts. This season we are focusing on Charity.

Acts of Charity Think about one act of charity you will do this week to show your love for someone. Complete the sentence.

Jesus loves me. He gave his life for me. I love Jesus.

This week I will _greet pepoel_

Hosanna

Gather and begin with the Sign of the Cross.

Leader: Hosanna, the King of Israel.

All: Hosanna. Hosanna.

Leader: Let us pray.

Bow your heads as the leader prays.

All: Amen.

Listen to God's Word

Leader: A reading from the holy Gospel according to John.

Read John 12:12-13.

The Gospel of the Lord.

All: Praise to you, Lord Jesus Christ.

Leader: Let us renew our baptismal promises.

All: Respond "I do" to the leader's questions.

Leader: Let us go out to praise the Lord.

All: Thanks be to God. Hosanna!

 Sing "Hosanna"

FAMILY+FAITH
LIVING AND LEARNING TOGETHER

TALKING ABOUT LENT >>>

Holy Week is the holiest week of the Church Year. It begins on Palm Sunday and continues until Evening Prayer on Easter Sunday. The Triduum or "three days" mark the most sacred time of Holy Week. It begins at sundown on Holy Thursday and ends at sundown on Easter Sunday. During these three days, the whole Church fasts and prays with anticipation and hope. On Holy Thursday, the assembly gathers for the washing of the feet and the Lord's Supper. This is a special Mass because it commemorates the institution of the Eucharist. At the end of the Mass, the altar and its surrounding area are stripped of ornamentation, in preparation for the solemn observances on Good Friday.

God's Word

 Read **John 12:12–16**, the story of Jesus' triumphal entrance into Jerusalem on Palm Sunday.

HELPING YOUR CHILD UNDERSTAND >>>
Holy Week

- At this age most children will get caught up in the experience of Holy Week as a sacred journey when you take the time to mark the days with moments of prayer or reading from a Children's Bible.

- Usually young children are curious and will have the most questions about Jesus' Death on the Cross. Do not emphasize the suffering of Jesus for children at this age. Talk with them about Jesus' Death as a sign of God's amazing love.

FEASTS OF THE SEASON >>>
Holy Thursday

Many families share a special meal on Holy Thursday before attending the evening Mass. It is appropriate to share hot cross buns or other special bread on the night when Jesus gave us the Bread of Life. Consider mentioning the meaning of the day in your blessing before the meal.

FAMILY PRAYER >>>

 On Good Friday, the Church venerates the cross. Make the Cross the focal point of your prayer this week and say the following together:

Lord by your Cross and Resurrection you have freed us. Have mercy on us. Amen.

For a multimedia glossary of Catholic Faith Words, Sunday readings, seasonal and Saint resources, and chapter activities go to **aliveinchrist.osv.com**.

He Is Risen

 Let Us Pray

Leader: Lord, God, bless us with Easter joy.

"This is the day that the LORD has made;
let us rejoice in it and be glad."
Psalm 118:24

All: Amen.

🕮 God's Word

The angel said to the women, "Do not be afraid! I know that you are seeking Jesus. He is not here, for he has been raised… go quickly and tell his disciples…"
Based on Matthew 28:5–7

❓ What Do You Wonder?

- Why did Jesus rise to new life?
- How does Jesus live in us?

Easter Joy

Why is Easter a time of joy and happiness?

Easter

The fifty days that the Church celebrates Jesus' Resurrection from the dead.

Jesus was dead, but three days later he rose from the dead to new life. Jesus was alive. What great power God showed! Jesus is risen! Now he lives in us!

Our Catholic Tradition

For more, go to page **368**

Celebrate Easter Color in the Easter egg.

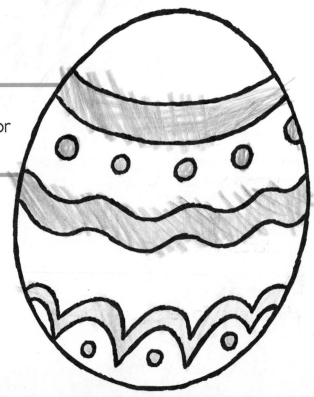

Signs of New Life After a long winter, the Earth returns to life in the spring. This is a sign of new life. This is what we celebrate during Easter, new life and hope. Check off the things in the list below that are signs of new life.

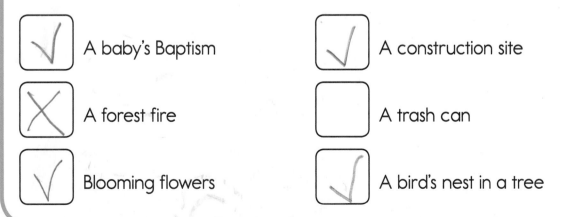

A baby's Baptism

A construction site

A forest fire

A trash can

Blooming flowers

A bird's nest in a tree

Our Catholic Life

© Our Sunday Visitor

When do you feel joyful? When someone is kind to you? When your favorite family member comes to see you? When you are kind to someone else? Joy is a good feeling. You can be joyful and bring joy to others.

Joy is one of the twelve Fruits of the Holy Spirit. It is a feeling of being happy just because of all God's wonderful gifts. Joy comes from knowing Jesus and loving him. Joy comes from being kind and sharing with others.

The season of Easter is a season of joy. During the Easter season, we celebrate the joy of Jesus' Resurrection from the dead. He lives! We sing Alleluia! We sing our joy.

Activity

Bringing Joy Draw a picture of something that brings you joy.

Let Us Pray

Celebrate Easter

Gather and begin with the Sign of the Cross.

Leader: Jesus is risen, alleluia.

All: Jesus is risen, alleluia.

Leader: Let us pray.

Bow your heads as the leader prays.

All: Amen.

Listen to God's Word

Leader: A reading from the holy Gospel according to John.

Read John 20:19–22.

The Gospel of the Lord.

All: Praise to you, Lord Jesus Christ.

Leader: Go out to celebrate new life, alleluia.

All: Thanks be to God, alleluia.

 Sing "Alleluia"

Allelu, allelu, alleluia!

FAMILY+FAITH
LIVING AND LEARNING TOGETHER

TALKING ABOUT EASTER >>>

On Easter morning, the Church rejoices. We celebrate as People of God who have received the gift of salvation. The celebration of the Easter season includes the fifty days following the Triduum. The Easter liturgies of these eight weeks reflect the joy of salvation in song and in action. The Alleluia not only returns to the repertoire, but also expresses wholeheartedly the joy of the Body of Christ. The Church renews their baptismal commitments in the sprinkling rite. The Gospels unpack the meaning of the Easter event and help the assembly to celebrate God's saving power.

God's Word

 Read **Matthew 28:1–10**, which describes the women's trip to the empty tomb on Easter morning and their conversation with the angel about Jesus' Resurrection.

HELPING YOUR CHILD UNDERSTAND >>>
Easter

- Young children usually enter easily into the joy of the Easter season.

- At this age most children will usually enter into the mystery of Easter through the Gospel stories of the events after the Resurrection.

- Generally, children this age do not understand that Jesus' body would look different after the Resurrection.

FEASTS OF THE SEASON >>>
Ascension Thursday

Ascension Thursday marks the Ascension of the Risen Christ to Heaven and is celebrated forty days after Easter. It is a Holy Day of Obligation. Sometimes dioceses move the celebration of the feast to the Sunday following Ascension Thursday, the Seventh Sunday of Easter.

FAMILY PRAYER >>>

 Say this prayer before your Sunday meal during the Easter season.

Leader: We joyfully sing your praises, Lord Jesus Christ, who on the day of your Resurrection was recognized by your disciples in the breaking of the bread. Remain here with us as we gratefully partake of these gifts, and at the banquet table in Heaven welcome us, who have welcomed you in your brothers and sisters, for you live and reign forever and ever. All: Amen.

For a multimedia glossary of Catholic Faith Words, Sunday readings, seasonal and Saint resources, and chapter activities go to **aliveinchrist.osv.com**.

Pentecost

 Let Us Pray

Leader: Come Holy Spirit.
Fill us with your power and love.
Help us follow Jesus.

"Bless the LORD, my soul! Hallelujah!"
Psalm 104:35b

All: Amen.

 God's Word

"Do you know that your body is a temple of the holy Spirit within you, whom you have from God, and that you are not your own? For you have been purchased at a price. Therefore glorify God in your body." 1 Corinthians 6:19–20

? What Do You Wonder?

- What is a Temple?
- How does the Holy Spirit help us?

The Holy Spirit

How did the Holy Spirit help the Apostles?

A cheer shows spirit. You cannot see spirit, but you know when people have it. You cannot see the Holy Spirit. The Holy Spirit is always with you.

After Jesus was raised from the dead, he sent the Holy Spirit. The Holy Spirit came to the Apostles in the form of wind and fire and helped them to remember what Jesus told them. This day is called Pentecost.

Underline how the Holy Spirit helped the Apostles.

Our Catholic Tradition
For more, go to page 359

Activity

Celebrate Pentecost When you enter your church for the celebration of Pentecost, you may see many decorations to remind you of the Holy Spirit. Below are symbols of the Holy Spirit. Write the names of the symbols in the space beside each picture.

Fire

dove

wind

Our Catholic Life

Aaron got up for school on time. He did what his mother asked him to do right away. He felt really good.

Peace is one of the twelve Fruits of the Holy Spirit. It is a feeling of calm that comes from doing the right things. When you feel peace, you know God is in your heart. You are a peacemaker when you follow Jesus' example.

At Pentecost we celebrate that Jesus has brought the message of peace to us. Our mission is to share his peace with others.

Fruits of the Holy Spirit

The twelve **Fruits of the Holy Spirit** are what others can see in us when we let the Holy Spirit work in our hearts. This season we are focusing on **Peace**

Activity

Peacemakers Place a check mark next to the examples of someone being a peacemaker.

 Sally asked Wendy and Kelly to stop arguing and to be kinder to each other. She hated to see her friends fighting.

 Christina didn't want Gabriela to sit with her and her friends on the bus so she put her book bag down in the empty spot next to her.

 Robbie hated when his older sister got to stay up later than him on the weekdays so he told his mother that she didn't finish her homework.

 When everyone in class ignored the new kid, Charlie walked up to him and introduced himself to Jake.

 **Let Us Pray**

Celebrate the Spirit

Gather and begin with the Sign of the Cross.

Leader: Come, Holy Spirit.

All: Fill our hearts with your love.

Leader: Let us pray.

Bow your heads as the leader prays.

All: Amen.

Listen to God's Word

Leader: A reading from the Acts of the Apostles.

Read Acts 2:1–4.

The word of the Lord.

All: Thanks be to God.

(You will be blessed with holy water as you
go forth.)

Leader: Let us go forth to live in God's Spirit
and share joy, peace, and love.

All: Thanks be to God.

 Sing "The Holy Spirit"

FAMILY+FAITH
LIVING AND LEARNING TOGETHER

TALKING ABOUT PENTECOST >>>

The Church celebrates the coming of the Holy Spirit on Pentecost. Pentecost occurs fifty days after Easter. It is often referred to as the birthday of the Church. On Pentecost, the sanctuary colors and priest's vestments are red symbolizing the fire of Pentecost and the empowerment of the Holy Spirit. In the Scripture readings, the liturgical music, and the gestures of the assembly, the Church celebrates God's empowering activity through the Gifts of the Holy Spirit.

God's Word

 Read **1 Corinthians 6:19–20**, which describes the dwelling of the Holy Spirit within us and our responsibility to respect our bodies.

HELPING YOUR CHILD UNDERSTAND >>>
Pentecost

- At this age, children will generally relate to the Holy Spirit as a guide and friend.
- Most children this age know what it is like to have spirit, and that knowledge is easily related to the Holy Spirit.
- At this age children usually have very vivid imaginations and will easily relate to the sights and sounds of the Pentecost story.

FEASTS OF THE SEASON >>>

Feast of Saint Philip Neri
May 26

Saint Philip Neri is an example of a holy person with a sense of humor. One time during prayer he felt a globe of light enter his mouth and sink into his heart. From that time on he had unending energy to serve God and he started speaking to people of all walks of life about God.

FAMILY PRAYER >>>

 Say this prayer together daily in the upcoming week.

Come Holy Spirit, fill us with the fire of your love that we may never tire of using your gifts to serve others and draw closer to you. Amen.

For a multimedia glossary of Catholic Faith Words, Sunday readings, seasonal and Saint resources, and chapter activities go to **aliveinchrist.osv.com**.

Units at a Glance

Revelation

Our Catholic Tradition

- God the Father is the Creator. (CCC, 317)

- God tells us about himself in the wonderful world that he made. (CCC, 319)

- We are God's children, made in his image and likeness. (CCC, 239, 353)

- God gave us life. He wants to be our friend. He wants us to be friends with others. (CCC, 356)

- God asks us to share his love with all people and to take care of his creation. (CCC, 357–358)

Our Catholic Life

- God's gifts of creation, most especially people, help us in many ways. (CCC, 306)

- We use the things God created to make things we need. (CCC, 307)

- We take care of ourselves because God loves us. (CCC, 2288)

What do we know about God?

Created by God

 Let Us Pray

Leader: Thank you, God, for making each one of us special.

You have examined me and you know me. You know everything I do.
You see me and you know all my actions.
Based on Psalm 139:1–3

All: God, help us know and love you. Amen.

God's Word

God, you created every part of me: you put me together...I praise you...everything you do is wonderful...you saw me before I was born.
Based on Psalm 139:13–15

 What Do You Wonder?

- Why did God create everything?
- How did God make everyone so different?

Getting Started

In this chapter you will learn how God created everything. You will also learn that God made humans to be his friends and wants us to know and love him.

Use the circle below to show some of the things you like in God's world.

© Our Sunday Visitor

Catholic Faith Words

Here are the vocabulary words for this chapter:

- Bible
- creation

In the empty spaces, draw four things that God made.

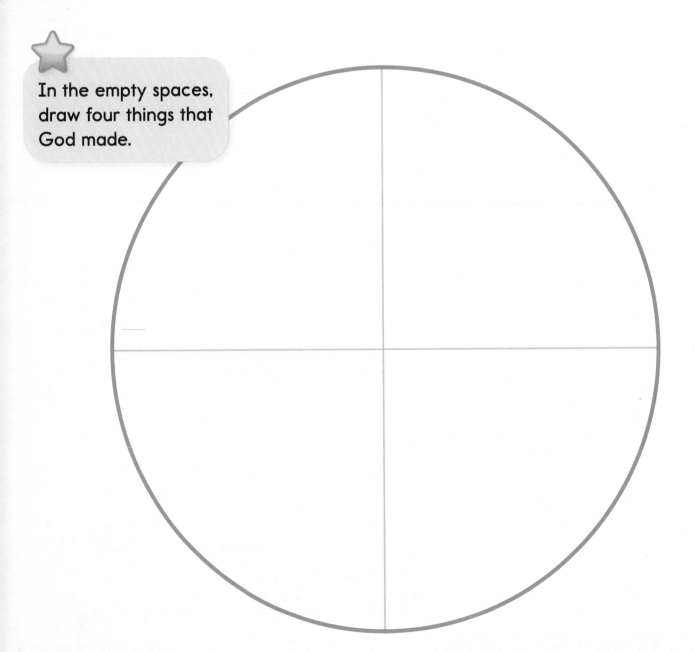

Show What God Made Trace the answers to the questions below to show some more of the things God made.

1. What shines in the sky?

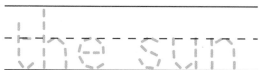
the sun

2. What grows big and tall and gives homes to birds?

trees

3. What grows from seeds and often smells good?

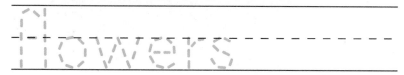
flowers

4. Who will God love forever and ever?

God's Creation

Who is the Creator of all things?

Our Catholic Tradition
For more, go to page 356

You are God's child. God knows you and loves you. The **Bible** is God's Word and has many stories about God's love for all of us.

Listen to this Bible story. It is about God and how he made Adam and Eve.

God's Word

The Garden of Eden

A very long time ago, God created the first man. God breathed into the man, and the man began to live. God loved the man and wanted him to be happy. God created a woman to be the man's partner. The man's name was Adam. The woman's name was Eve.

Based on Genesis 2:7–22

© Our Sunday Visitor

Draw yourself into the picture of the things that God made.

God Gives Life

God made everything. All his **creation** is good. God is our Father and the Creator. He gave you life.

Activity

Think Trace the word that tells what everything that God made is called.

_____

creation

Share your answer with a classmate.

Catholic Faith Words

Bible the Word of God written in human words. The Bible is the holy book of the Church.

creation everything made by God

God Loves You

Who wants to be your friend?

Those who love you know you best. God knows you better than anyone knows you. He wants you to know him, too.

God loves you very much. He is your friend. God wants you to be friends with others, too.

➤ **What is one thing you know about God?**

In the picture circle two of your favorite things that God made.

God's World

God created a wonderful
world. It is filled with lots of good things.

There are mountains and rivers,
and fish in the stream,

Birds soaring high and
good things to dream.

There are flowers and
forests and puppy dogs, too,

But the best thing of all is
that God made people, too.

Activity

Trace the Word

God _loves_ you!

69

Our Catholic Life

How do we use some of the things God created?

God made so many wonderful things. God's gifts are all around you. They help you in many ways.

Draw a line from the pictures to the matching words.

Gifts God Gives Us

God made the sun and the for us.   •   • birds

God gave us flowers and .   •   • moon

God made trees that grow .   •   • friends

God gave you to play with.   •   • families

Best of all, he made  to love you.   •   • fruit

People of Faith

Blessed Fra Angelico, 1387–1455

Blessed Fra Angelico was an artist who painted pictures of Jesus, Mary, the Saints, and the angels. One of his most famous paintings shows the Angel Gabriel visiting Mary. Fra Angelico was asked by the Pope to decorate a special little chapel in the Vatican. Even today, many people come to see his paintings.

February 18

Discuss: Where do you see pictures of Jesus?

Learn more about Blessed Fra Angelico at **aliveinchrist.osv.com**

Activity

Tell What gifts of creation are the people in the picture enjoying?

Color Finish coloring the picture.

 **Let Us Pray**

Prayer of Praise

Gather and begin with the Sign of the Cross.

Leader: For the sun and the moon way up in the sky,

All: Praise God!

Leader: For flowers that grow, for birds flying by,

All: Praise God!

Leader: For trees and for fruit that is yummy to share,

All: Praise God!

Leader: For children and families who show love and care,

All: Praise God!

Leader: For all the great things God's love made to be,

All: Praise God!

Leader: For all of creation and that includes me,

All: Praise God!

 Sing "God Is a Part of My Life"

Chapter 1 Review

A **Work with Words** Trace the letters to tell about God's gifts.

1. God made  Adam

and Eve.

2. God created everything.

3. God loves me!

B **Check Understanding** Circle the word that finishes the sentence.

4. God is our ____.

    Creator   pet

5. The ____ is God's Word.

    Bible   Garden

Go to aliveinchrist.osv.com
for an interactive review.

FAMILY + FAITH

LIVING AND LEARNING TOGETHER

YOUR CHILD LEARNED >>>

This chapter teaches about God's gift of creation and his love for us. He made us to know and love him.

God's Word

 Read **Psalm 139:13–15** to find out how each one of us is special to God.

Catholics Believe

• God created everything. All that he made is good.

• God knows and loves everyone.

To learn more, go to the *Catechism of the Catholic Church* #295, 299 at **usccb.org**.

People of Faith

This week, your child met Blessed Fra Angelico. He was an innovative painter who used his gifts and talents to honor God.

CHILDREN AT THIS AGE >>>

How They Understand Our Creation by God Many first graders have not yet asked themselves how they came to be. They know from photos and stories that they used to be babies, but it is difficult for them to picture a time when they did not exist. For this reason, when they are taught that God made them, they might accept this idea without much thought. As they grow and learn more about how new life comes about, they will integrate this information through an understanding that people, like their parents, cooperate with God to bring new life into the world.

CONSIDER THIS >>>

Can you ever completely know someone?

No matter how long we know someone it would be foolish to say we know that person completely. God creates each of us with the capacity to know him. When we open our hearts we come to know him in many ways. "In the encounter of God with Moses, God reveals himself as 'I AM WHO I AM.' These words reveal... God...as the source of all that is, but who he is will be revealed still further as he continues his loving work for his people" (*USCCA, p. 13*).

LET'S TALK >>>

• Ask your child to name who made everything in creation.

• Share with your child your favorite part of God's creation.

LET'S PRAY >>>

 Dear God, you show us your love when you make beautiful things. Help us to always love you, as Blessed Fra Angelico did. Amen.

For a multimedia glossary of Catholic Faith Words, Sunday readings, seasonal and Saint resources, and chapter activities go to **aliveinchrist.osv.com**.

God's Gifts for Us

❤ Let Us Pray

Leader: God, we thank you for all the wonderful gifts you give to us.

"O LORD our Lord,
how awesome is your name through
all the earth!"   Psalm 8:2

All: Help us to see all your gifts. Amen.

📖 God's Word

God created all the plants and flowers, all the animals that walk on the earth, fly in the sky, and swim in the waters. He said, "I created all kinds of food for you to eat." And God was pleased with what he saw.

Based on Genesis 1:11–31

❓ What Do You Wonder?

- How did God think of all the things he made?
- Why did God make bugs?

Getting Started

In this chapter you will learn that all of God's creation is a gift to us. You will also learn that people use God's gifts in the world to make the things we need.

Use the chart below to show the different ways you can thank God.

Match the actions in the pictures to the different ways you can thank God for his gifts.

Ways to Thank God

Taking care of creation

Praying

Showing love

Catholic Faith Words

Here are the vocabulary words for this chapter:

- Jesus
- praise
- thanksgiving

Activity

God's Gifts God's gifts include people, animals, food, a place to live, a place to learn, and all of the things we need to live.

Draw one of God's gifts that you are thankful for and describe it to a classmate.

Gifts from God

What gifts has God given to us?

God gives you a very, very big gift.

Stretch your arms wide. God's gift is bigger than that!

God's gift is too big to wrap. It is so big that no ribbon can be tied around it.

God gives you the world. He filled the world with many gifts! And his greatest gift is his Son, **Jesus**.

We **praise** God for these gifts.

Catholic Faith Words

Jesus the name of the Son of God who became man

praise giving God honor and thanks because he is God

Circle three gifts in God's world that you want to learn more about.

God Made the World

God made many good things. Before God made Adam and Eve, he made the world. He made the world to show his love.

☧ God's Word

The Story of Creation

Long ago, God made the sky, the earth and the seas. But the earth was empty. There were no trees to climb. No flowers swayed in the breeze. No birds to fly in the air.

So the Lord God created a beautiful world. God said: "Let the earth bring forth every kind of living creature: tame animals, crawling things, and every kind of wild animal." Then, birds flew in the sky. Many animals lived on the earth. And fish and whales swam in the seas. God saw that it was good.   **Based on Genesis 1:6–25**

Activity

Think What are some of God's gifts that you would like to bring to your next class?

Share Talk about these gifts with your class.

Made to Help Us

How do God's gifts help us?

God made people to love. We can learn something about God's love for us by the things he made. He gives us what we need to live and be happy.

We use God's gifts to make other things we need. Wood for houses comes from trees. Food is made from animals or plants.

Trace the words that tell how God's gift of people helps the world.

God's Gifts Help the World

God's Gift	How It Helps
	gives light at night
	we make paper from it
	makes the day bright
	we love

Thank God

Everything around you is a gift from God. We can show God we are grateful for all he's given us. We call this **thanksgiving**.

- We can pray to show God thanks.

- We can remember that all we have comes from God.

- We take care of and share these gifts.

- We can tell our family and friends "thank you" for the things they do.

Catholic Faith Words

thanksgiving giving thanks to God for all he has given us

Activity

Give Thanks Color the x's blue and the o's green to tell God something special.

Our Catholic Life

How do people use the things God made?

God gave people many gifts to use. People use God's gifts to make other things they need.

Our Catholic Tradition

For more, go to page 380

You can use God's gifts to make the food you eat.

Pancake mix is made from flour.

Milk comes from a cow.

Eggs come from a chicken.

All together they make yummy pancakes!

People of Faith

Saint Nicholas, 270–310

Saint Nicholas was a bishop. One night he went to the house of a poor family and threw a bag of gold coins in an open window. The family wanted to thank Nicholas, but he told them to thank God instead. Nicholas liked giving gifts in secret. People still give gifts on his feast day. Saint Nicholas is the patron Saint of children.

December 6

Discuss: What gift can you give to your family and friends today?

Learn more about Saint Nicholas at **aliveinchrist.osv.com**

Activity

Thank You, God Color the places where you can say thank you to God this week for giving us so many gifts.

 **Let Us Pray**

Prayer of Thanksgiving

Gather and begin with the Sign of the Cross.

Leader: Let us give thanks to God for all his gifts.

All: For your gift of the Earth,
Thank you, God.

For your gift of plants and trees,
Thank you, God.

For your gift of animals, Thank you, God.

For your gift of food, Thank you, God.

For your gift of people, Thank you, God.

For your gift of me, Thank you, God.

For your whole-wide-world of gifts,
Thank you, God.

 Sing "And It Was Good"

And it was good, good, very, very good,
and it was good, good, very, very good,
and it was good, good, very, very good,
it was very, very, very good.
Text and music: Jack Miffleton. © 1990, OCP. All rights reserved.

Chapter 2 Review

A **Work with Words** Fill in the circle beside the correct answer.

1. Showing God you are grateful for what he has given us is called ____.

⬤ thanksgiving   ◯ happiness

2. God created the world to ____.

◯ do some work   ⬤ show his love

3. The name of the Son of God who became man is ____.

⬤ Jesus   ◯ John

4. Giving God honor and thanks because he is good is called ____.

◯ prayer   ⬤ praise

B **Check Understanding** Draw one thing that God created.

5.

FAMILY+FAITH
LIVING AND LEARNING TOGETHER

YOUR CHILD LEARNED >>>

This chapter explores how God gives us what we need to live and be happy. We can thank God for his gifts in many ways.

God's Word

 Read **Genesis 1:11–31** to find out about the many gifts God created for us to enjoy

Catholics Believe

- God's world is a gift to you.
- You can learn about God and his love by looking at the world he made.

To learn more, go to the *Catechism of the Catholic Church* #315, 319 at **usccb.org**.

People of Faith

This week, your child met Saint Nicholas. Saint Nicholas spent his life helping the needy and is the model for our Santa Claus.

CHILDREN AT THIS AGE >>>

How They Understand God's Creation First graders are very concrete thinkers—they know and understand the things they perceive with their senses. For this reason, many children understand God in the context of what he has made. Knowing that God made the trees, flowers, animals, oceans, people, and everything in the world teaches them that God is very big and powerful. God's identity is still a mystery for them, but creation becomes for them the "evidence" that God is real.

CONSIDER THIS >>>

Have you ever had the feeling that someone should be thanked?

There are moments of awe in everyone's life that break through the "ordinary." At these moments we have a sense of the transcendent. "Augustine tells us that God spoke with a vigorous voice. 'You called, you shouted, and you broke through my deafness. You breathed your fragrance on me.... I have tasted you, now I hunger and thirst for more' (*The Confessions*, bk. 10, no. 27)" (*USCCA, p. 346*).

LET'S TALK >>>

- Ask your child to name one way we use some of the things God made.
- Talk about a time you were really thankful for God's action in your life. What are some ways people in your family show they are thankful?

LET'S PRAY >>>

 Saint Nicholas, help us give generously to the poor like you did. Amen.

 For a multimedia glossary of Catholic Faith Words, Sunday readings, seasonal and Saint resources, and chapter activities go to **aliveinchrist.osv.com**.

Made to Care

 Let Us Pray

Leader: God, thank you for teaching us how to care for all of creation.

"Let everything that has breath give praise to the LORD!" Psalm 150:6

All: Help us care for the things you have made. Amen.

 God's Word

God created human beings and said: "I am putting you in charge to care for all that I created." God looked at everything that he had made, and he found it very good.

Based on Genesis 1:27–31

? What Do You Wonder?

- How can you take care of God's creation?
- Why does God want people to care for what he made?

87

Getting Started

Catholic Faith Words

Here is the vocabulary word for this chapter:

• image of God

In this chapter you will learn that humans are the most special part of God's creation. You will also learn that God wants everyone to help care for the things God made.

Use the chart below to show what living things need.

 Circle the things that plants, animals, and people need to live.

What Living Things Need

What Plants Need	What Animals Need	What People Need
light	hair	cartoons
crayons	air	food
water	fertilizer	shelter
ears	food	cake

Activity

A Special Part of Creation God made people to be a special part of creation. Look at the pictures below. What makes the people in the pictures special?

1. Friendship together all the time

2. Playing together.

Tell a classmate about some special things you can do.

In God's Image

How are you a part of God's creation?

God made people in his image, to be like him. Find out how we are special parts of creation.

How Are You Special?

Josh and his mother were making cookies. Josh held up a piece of dough. "First I want to make a head, then the arms and body…the legs are last. Look! I made a person! He is just like me!"

Josh's mother laughed. "He does look like you, Josh. But he is not just like you. How are you different?"

Catholic Faith Words

image of God the likeness of God that is in all human beings because we are created by him

Josh thought for a minute. "I am real. I can think, play, learn at school, and pray. I can hug you. And you can't eat me!"

"That's right, Josh," his mother said.

Gifts in Creation

Josh made a cookie that looked like him. But it was not really like him. God made all people in his image. We were all made in the **image of God** to be like him. That makes people the most special part of creation. We are each unique but all share God's image. This is why we respect all people of every age.

 Underline two gifts that are inside of each person.

Creation is full of gifts from God. Some gifts are part of the world. Other gifts are inside of each person. Being able to think and make choices are two of those gifts.

Activity

Think Draw one thing about yourself that shows you are a sign of God's love.

Share Talk with a classmate about what you like about this gift.

© Our Sunday Visitor

God's Command

What does God ask you to do?

Our Catholic Tradition
For more, go to page **358**

Of all God's creatures, only humans can do things like make choices and show love. God the Father created us to know his love and share in his work. Listen to what he asked Adam and Eve to do.

Circle what God asked Adam and Eve to do.

Everything on Earth is part of God's creation.

 God's Word

Take Care of What I've Given You

God made Adam and Eve to be like him. He said to them, "Have children to fill the earth. Use the earth for what you need. Here are plants with seeds, and animals, and birds. Take care of all that I have given you."

Based on Genesis 1:26–30

Show Love

God told Adam and Eve to care for his creation. God asks you to be a good caretaker, someone who treats his creation with care and respect. When you care for living things, you show your love for God. Caring is a way to thank God for all that he has given you.

Activity

Fill it In Trace the words to complete the sentence that tells what God asked Adam and Eve to do.

Take care of all that I have given you.

Share your answer with a classmate.

Our Catholic Life

How do you help take care of yourself?

You are one of God's greatest gifts! He made your body and your mind. God loves and cares for you very much. He wants you to help take care of yourself.

Check off the things you like to do best.

Take Care of Yourself

Care for Your Body	Care for Your Mind
☐ Eat good foods.	☐ Listen to stories.
☐ Keep your hair, teeth, and body clean.	☐ Do your best in school.
☐ Play and get exercise.	☐ Make something.
☐ Get enough sleep at night.	☐ Learn to do a new thing.

People of Faith

Saint Albert the Great, 1206–1280

Saint Albert was a German priest. He was very smart. He liked to learn about God's world. He looked carefully at spider webs. He studied the stars and the way they move. He spent hours looking at plants and watching animals. He even wrote a book on how to take care of falcons! Because of all the things he knew, he was given the title "the Great." Saint Albert loved all creation because it was made by God.

November 15

Discuss: Name one thing you like to look at when you are outside in God's world.

Learn more about Saint Albert at **aliveinchrist.osv.com**

Activity

Tell how you use the objects below to take care of yourself.

Name one way you will take care of yourself this week.

Let Us Pray

Prayer of Praise and Thanks

Gather and begin with the Sign of the Cross.

Leader: God made a wonderful world!
Give thanks to God for his wonderful world.

All: Thank you, thank you, thank you, God.

Leader: For pets and trees and carrots and peas,
And birds that fly and sing.

All: Thank you, thank you, thank you, God.

Leader: We sing our thanks and praise to you,
Every day and night!

We'll care for all that you have made,
We'll try with all our might!

All: Sing "All Things Bright and Beautiful"

All things bright and beautiful,
all creatures great and small,
all things wise and wonderful:
the Lord God made them all.
Text based on Ecclesiastes 3:11;
Cecil Frances Alexander. Music by ROYAL OAK.

Chapter 3 Review

A **Work with Words** Look at each picture. Draw a line from the word or words to the picture that explains it.

Column A   Column B

1. Image of God

2. Caretaker

3. Adam and Eve

B **Check Understanding** Trace the words to name one way you can take care of your body and one way you can take care of your mind.

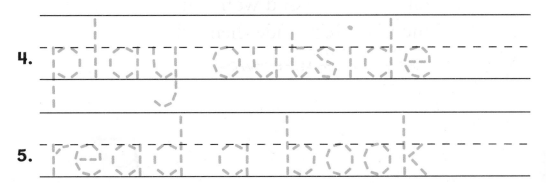

4. play outside

5. read a book

Go to **aliveinchrist.osv.com** for an interactive review.

FAMILY+FAITH

LIVING AND LEARNING TOGETHER

YOUR CHILD LEARNED >>>

This chapter explains what it means to be made in God's image and how people have a special role in taking care of creation.

God's Word

 Read **Genesis 1:27–31** to learn about how God asks us to take care of everyone and everything that was created.

Catholics Believe

• All creation is a gift from God. Humans are the most special part of creation.

• Everyone must help care for God's gifts.

To learn more, go to the *Catechism of the Catholic Church* #374–379 at **usccb.org**.

People of Faith

This week, your child met Saint Albert the Great. Albert was one of the world's first scientists.

CHILDREN AT THIS AGE >>>

How They Understand Being Stewards of God's Creation
At the beginning of the school year, many first graders are still very much in what developmental theorists describe as the "egocentric" stage of development. They see the world as revolving around them and have difficulty seeing things from the perspective of others. Consequently, they have no difficulty grasping the idea that God made the world for them and that they have some responsibility in caring for what God has given them. Your child may need help, though, to discover practical ways in which he or she can be a good steward of God's creation.

CONSIDER THIS >>>

How do children distinguish between what they want and what they need?

This is a serious challenge when outside factors convince them that they need more than they really do. When Jesus proclaimed the eight Beatitudes he stated that "poverty of spirit would enable us to inherit the Kingdom of God. In other words, the first step on the road to joy begins with a healthy detachment from material goods" (*USCCA, p. 449*). If we want our children to know that joy, we must teach detachment to material goods through our own example.

LET'S TALK >>>

• Ask your child to name one thing people can do that the rest of God's creation cannot.

• Tell your child what makes him or her special to you.

LET'S PRAY >>>

 Saint Albert, help us take care of all living things in the world, including the plants, the animals, and the people. Amen.

For a multimedia glossary of Catholic Faith Words, Sunday readings, seasonal and Saint resources, and chapter activities go to **aliveinchrist.osv.com**.

A **Work with Words** Fill in the circle beside the correct answer.

1. ____ made the world.

   ● God   ○ You

2. All ____ is a gift from God.

   ○ noise   ● creation

3. The ____ is the Word of God written in human words.

   ● Bible   ○ world

4. ____ is the Son of God who became man.

   ○ John   ● Jesus

5. All people are made in the image of ____.

   ● God   ○ Adam

B **Check Understanding** Draw a line from each picture to the phrase that best describes it.

Column A   Column B

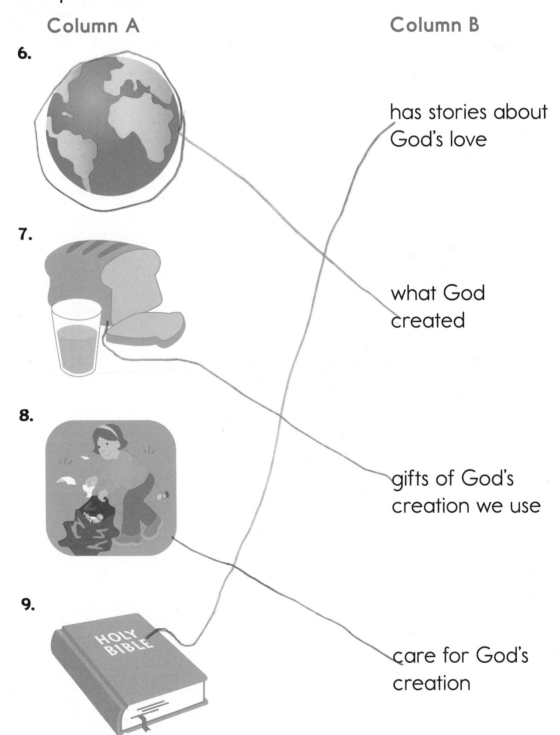

6.

has stories about
God's love

7.

what God
created

8.

gifts of God's
creation we use

9.

care for God's
creation

© Our Sunday Visitor

C **Make Connections** Draw a picture of yourself taking care of or using one thing God made.

10.

Trinity

Our Catholic Tradition

- The Holy Trinity is one God in three Divine Persons—God the Father, the Son, and the Holy Spirit. (CCC, 234)

- God the Father is the First Divine Person of the Holy Trinity. He loves and takes care of us. (CCC, 239)

- Jesus is the Second Divine Person of the Holy Trinity. He is the Son of God. (CCC, 262)

- The Holy Spirit is the Third Divine Person of the Holy Trinity. God sent his Holy Spirit to be with us always and to help us share God's love. (CCC, 263)

Our Catholic Life

- God is love, and we share in the love of the Father, Son, and Holy Spirit. (CCC, 257)

- The Holy Family teaches us about family life, honoring God, work, and love. (CCC, 533)

- We learn from the Bible how to show love for God and others. (CCC, 131)

What does the Bible teach us about Jesus?

The Holy Trinity

 Let Us Pray

Leader: Your name is holy, O Lord our God.

"Give to the LORD the glory due his name.
Bow down before the LORD's holy splendor!" Psalm 29:2

All: May we always remember that your name is holy. And so we pray: In the name of the Father, and of the Son, and of the Holy Spirit. Amen.

 God's Word

Jesus said to the disciples: "…Go, therefore, and make disciples of all nations, baptizing them in the name of the Father, and of the Son, and of the holy Spirit, teaching them to observe all that I have commanded you."
Matthew 28:19–20

? What Do You Wonder?

- Why were you given your name?
- What does your name mean?

Getting Started

Catholic Faith Words

Here are the vocabulary words for this chapter:

- God the Father
- Son of God
- Holy Trinity

In this chapter you will learn that the Holy Trinity is God the Father, God the Son, and God the Holy Spirit, the one God in three Divine Persons. You will also learn that Jesus is the Son of God and a friend to us. God asks us to be friends with one another and be kind to each other.

Use the chart below to show what you already know about good friends.

Check off the things that good friends do.

Things Good Friends Do

✓ Help each other	✓ Share toys
✓ Play	Scream at each other
Fight	✓ Laugh together
Tell lies	✓ Give hugs

Father, Son, and Holy Spirit Saint Patrick used
the three leafed clover to help explain the Trinity.
Color the X's green and the O's blue to find the
hidden symbol.

Helping Others

How can we be nice to others?

God always wants you to be nice to other people. Lion and Mouse have a problem. Read to find out how they solve the problem.

The Lion and the Mouse

A mighty lion was fast asleep in the woods. Mouse thought Lion was a rock. She ran up his back. Lion woke at once.

He grabbed poor Mouse's tail.

"How dare you wake me up?" he roared. "I am going to eat you!"

"Oh, please," Mouse said. "Let me go. Someday I will repay you."

1. Underline two things Lion did to Mouse.

2. Circle how Mouse helped Lion.

"Don't be silly!" Lion roared. "How will you repay me? You are just a little mouse." Then he laughed. "All right, go on," he said.

He put Mouse down and she ran away quickly.

Many days had passed. Mouse ran by that same place. Mouse heard an awful roar. She soon found Lion caught in a net.

Quickly Mouse ran to the net. She chewed through the rope and set Lion free!

"Thank you," roared Lion.

"You are welcome," said Mouse. "Now I hope that you can see what a big help small friends can be!"

Brothers, sisters, and friends can help each other do big things.

Activity

Think What did Lion learn about being a friend?

Small friends can be a big help.

Share Who has been a good friend to you and why?

God Is Love

How does the Holy Trinity show love?

God cares for you like a good friend does. He loves you like a loving parent or grandparent does. He loves you even more than you can imagine.

You call him **God the Father**. You see his love in creation. You learn about his love from Jesus, the **Son of God**.

God the Father sent his Son to Earth to show people his love.

Catholic Faith Words

God the Father the First Divine Person of the Holy Trinity

Son of God a name for Jesus that tells you God is his Father. The Son of God is the Second Divine Person of the Holy Trinity.

 God's Word

The Way to the Father

One of the Apostles said to Jesus, "Master, show us the Father." Jesus said to him, "…Whoever has seen me has seen the Father." Based on John 14:8–9

The Holy Trinity

God the Father, God the Son, and God the Holy Spirit are the **Holy Trinity**. The Holy Trinity is the one God in three Divine Persons.

- Sometimes we say God or Lord when we pray to God the Father, from whom all things come.

- Jesus showed God's love by teaching, healing, and loving others.

- God the Holy Spirit helps you know and love Jesus and his Father.

Catholic Faith Words

Holy Trinity the one God in three Divine Persons—God the Father, God the Son, and God the Holy Spirit

Activity

Trace the Word Trace the word to find the name for the three Divine Persons in one God. Then color in the signs of the Trinity.

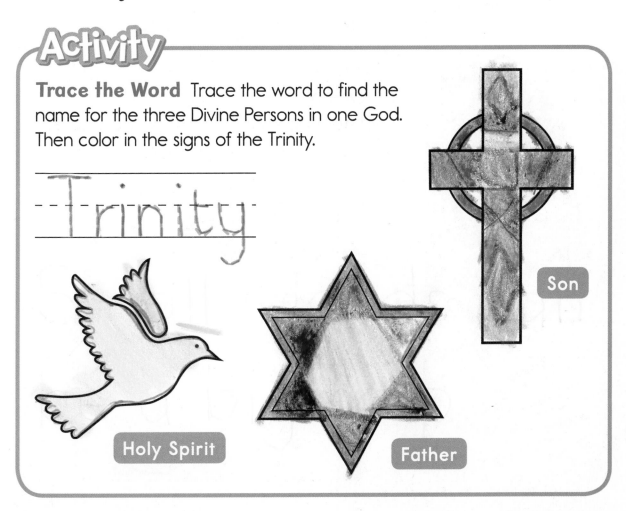

Trinity

Holy Spirit

Father

Son

Our Catholic Life

What do we know about God?

Jesus taught people some important things about God. The most important thing he taught others is that God loves everyone.

Circle the words Father, Son, and Holy Spirit.

Father, Son, and Holy Spirit

- God made all things, and cares for creation as our loving Father.
- God the Father sent his own Son, Jesus, to save all people, because he loves us.
- God sent his Holy Spirit to be with us always, because he loves us.

God the Father, God the Son, and God the Holy Spirit are the Holy Trinity.

Here is a way to remember what you know about the Trinity.

Father + Son + Holy Spirit

= 1 God

= Love

Our Catholic Tradition

For more, go to page 358

People of Faith

Saint Patrick, 387–493

Saint Patrick was kidnapped by pirates when he was just a boy. They took him to Ireland to be a slave. After six years, Patrick escaped and went back to his family. Years later, he returned to Ireland as a priest. He showed people a shamrock to explain the Holy Trinity: one God in three Divine Persons.

March 17

Discuss: How is the Sign of the Cross also the sign of the Holy Trinity?

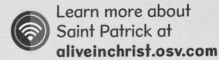

Learn more about Saint Patrick at **aliveinchrist.osv.com**

© Our Sunday Visitor

Activity

Fill It In Fill in the blank with the name of the correct Person of the Holy Trinity.

1. My name is Jesus. I taught people about God, my Father.

    I am God the Son.

2. I am with you always to help you share God's love.

    I am God the Holy Spirit.

3. I made the whole world, and I love and care for all people.

    I am God the Father.

111

Prayer of Praise

Gather and begin with the Sign of the Cross.

▶ **All:** Sing "The Sign of the Cross"

In the name of the Father,
and of the Son,
and of the Holy Spirit,
Amen.

Leader: Glory be to the Father,

All: Glory be to the Father,

Leader: and to the Son,

All: and to the Son,

Leader: and to the Holy Spirit:

All: and to the Holy Spirit:

Leader: as it was in the beginning, is now,
and will be forever.

All: as it was in the beginning
is now,
and ever shall be
world without end.
Amen.

Chapter 4 Review

A **Work with Words** Circle the correct answers.

1. Jesus is the <u>Son</u> of God.

(Son)   Father

2. Who are the three Divine Persons of the Holy Trinity?

The Three Kings   (Father, Son, and Holy Spirit)

3. God is our ____ who loves and cares for us.

cousin   (Father)

B **Check Understanding** Trace the letters to complete the sentence.

4. There are three Divine Persons in the

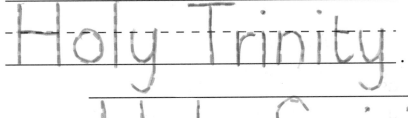

Holy Trinity.

5. God the

Holy Spirit

helps you know and love Jesus and the Father.

Go to **aliveinchrist.osv.com** for an interactive review.

FAMILY+FAITH

LIVING AND LEARNING TOGETHER

YOUR CHILD LEARNED >>>

This chapter introduces the Holy Trinity, the one God in three Divine Persons, and explains each Divine Person of God, what they do, and how they relate to one another.

God's Word

 Read **Matthew 28:19–20** as a family. Talk about how each of you helps others learn about God.

Catholics Believe

- The Holy Trinity is God the Father, God the Son, and God the Holy Spirit.

- Jesus is the Son of God who came to show the Father's love and bring us closer to him.

To learn more, go to the *Catechism of the Catholic Church* #253–254 at **usccb.org**.

People of Faith

This week, your child met Saint Patrick. He used a common plant, the shamrock, to explain the profound mystery of the Holy Trinity.

CHILDREN AT THIS AGE >>>

How They Understand God as Trinity

The Holy Trinity is the most basic mystery of our faith, but it is still a mystery, even for us as adults. Many Catholic first graders have heard and said the words of the Sign of the Cross countless times. They are accustomed to hearing about God the Father, God the Son, and God the Holy Spirit. Still, your child may have particular difficulty understanding how God can be one and yet also three. This is a mystery that will continue to unfold as he or she grows in faith and in relationship with God.

CONSIDER THIS >>>

What did you discover about love when your child was first placed in your arms?

Did you feel indescribable love? That experience of love begins in the heart of God, for God is love. "When a family becomes a school of virtue and a community of love, it is an image of the loving communion of the Father, Son, and Holy Spirit. It is then an icon of the Trinity" (*USCCA, p. 377*).

LET'S TALK >>>

- Ask your child to name the three Divine Persons of the Holy Trinity.

- Show your child how we honor the Holy Trinity when we make the Sign of the Cross at the beginning and end of prayers.

LET'S PRAY >>>

 Saint Patrick, help us teach others about God the Father, God the Son, and God the Holy Spirit in the Holy Trinity. Amen.

 For a multimedia glossary of Catholic Faith Words, Sunday readings, seasonal and Saint resources, and chapter activities go to **aliveinchrist.osv.com**.

The Holy Family

 Let Us Pray

Leader: Thank you, God, for our families.

How good and how pleasant it is,
when brothers dwell together as one!
Psalm 133:1

All: Help us to see your love and kindness in
our families. Amen.

🕮 God's Word

Joseph was told in a dream to take Mary
and Jesus to Galilee. They went to live there in
the town of Nazareth. So God's promise came
true…"He shall be called a Nazorean."
Based on Matthew 2:19–23

❓ What Do You Wonder?

• What was it like to live in
Nazareth?

• Did Jesus have to obey his
parents?

Getting Started

In this chapter you will learn that Jesus Christ is both true God and true man. You will also learn that Jesus grew up in the Holy Family.

Use the chart below to show what you know about the Holy Family.

© Our Sunday Visitor

 Match the pictures with the names of the members of the Holy Family.

The Holy Family

Jesus

Mary

Joseph

Catholic **Faith Words**

Here are the vocabulary words for this chapter:

- Holy Family
- Mary

Activity

Your Family Draw or write about your family. Who are the members of your family?

Family Love

How can families show love?

God the Father loves all families. Meet the families who live on Green Street.

Tyler's Family

Tyler's Dad moved away, and Tyler is sad. Having an uncle to talk to makes Tyler feel glad.

Lainey's Family

"Let's read this email from your Gram," says Dad to Lainey.

"She says she is coming to visit soon."

David's Family

There's David and Mama and Papa, too, on a picnic in the park.

"Fetch the tennis ball, Rocky," David says.

Rocky chases after the ball with a happy bark.

Activity

Think Draw one way your family shows love.

Share Tell one way your family shares God's love.

Jesus' Family

What was Jesus' family like?

Long ago, Jesus was born into a family. Jesus lived with **Mary**, his Mother, and his foster father, Joseph. They lived in a town called Nazareth. Jesus, Mary, and Joseph are called the **Holy Family**.

Our Catholic Tradition For more, go to page 361

Jesus is the Son of God. Jesus is also human. He is like you in almost every way. Jesus shows you how to live. He teaches you about God's love.

Catholic Faith Words

Mary the Mother of Jesus, the Mother of God. She is also called "Our Lady" because she is our Mother and the Mother of the Church.

Holy Family the name for the human family of Jesus, Mary, and Joseph

A Day in Nazareth

All families can share God's love. When Jesus was your age, he showed God's love in his family.

 God's Word

The Boy Jesus

Jesus obeyed his family. He became wise and good. Jesus grew strong. God was pleased with him and so were the people.

Based on Luke 2:51–52

This is what could have happened when Jesus was young.

- Following Jewish custom, the family begins the day with a prayer.

- Mary bakes bread for breakfast.

- Joseph makes a chair for his neighbors.

- They spend time together as a family.

 Underline some things the Holy Family did that you do with your family.

Activity

Act Out Family Life What are some things the Holy Family might have done together? With a classmate, act out something families can do to show God's love.

Our Catholic Life

What was it like for Jesus when he was growing up?

Jesus grew up in a human family. He and his family probably did many of the same things together that you and your family do.

Match the pictures of the Holy Family with the correct actions.

Doing Chores

Traveling

Celebrating Holidays

People of Faith

Zechariah, Elizabeth, and John, first century

Elizabeth was Mary's cousin. She was married to Zechariah. They did not have children. One day an angel appeared to Zechariah when he was praying. The angel told him that he and Elizabeth would have a son named John. Elizabeth and Zechariah were very happy. When John grew up, he was filled with the Holy Spirit.

November 5

Discuss: How are you filled with the Holy Spirit?

 Learn more about Zechariah, Elizabeth, and John at **aliveinchrist.osv.com**

Activity

Draw Your Family
Draw a picture of your family doing something that the Holy Family might have done together.

MY FAMILY

Pray with God's Word

Gather and begin with the Sign of the Cross.

Leader: Today we learned about the Holy Family. Mary, Joseph, and Jesus help us to act with love in our families.

All: Thank you, Mary, for being the Mother of Jesus. Thank you, Joseph, for taking care of Jesus.

Leader: Let us listen to the Word of God. A reading from the holy Gospel according to Luke.

Read Luke 2:27–33.

All: Praise to you, Lord Jesus Christ.

Leader: Thank you, Jesus, for loving your family and thank you for our families. Help us to live with great love.

All: Amen.

 Sing "Joseph Was a Good Man"

A **Work with Words** Trace the words to complete the sentences.

1. **Mary** is the Mother of Jesus.

2. Jesus is the Son of God and he is also **human**.

3. Mark an X next to the things Jesus might have done with his family.

[X] pray [X] talk [X] visit

[X] eat [ ] play [X] help

4. Jesus, Mary, and Joseph are called the **Holy Family**.

B **Check Understanding** Circle ways you can help your family.

5.

Go to aliveinchrist.osv.com for an interactive review.

FAMILY+FAITH
LIVING AND LEARNING TOGETHER

YOUR CHILD LEARNED >>>

This chapter focuses on God's love for all families and the things the Holy Family did or could have done together.

God's Word

 Read **Mark 10:13–16** to see how Jesus wants us to care for children and families.

Catholics Believe

• Jesus is both true God and true man.

• Jesus, Mary, and Joseph are the Holy Family.

To learn more, go to the *Catechism of the Catholic Church* #531–534 at **usccb.org**.

People of Faith

This week, your child met Zechariah, Elizabeth, and John. These relatives of Jesus trusted God to direct their lives.

CHILDREN AT THIS AGE >>>

How They Understand the Holy Family When first graders hear that Jesus was once a child their age, it's natural for them to picture him in a family very much like their own. Just like they need someone to take care of them as they grow, so did Jesus. And it's important for them to realize that even Jesus had to listen to his mom and dad and follow their rules. Make these important connections to show your child that Jesus was like them in all things except he did not sin.

CONSIDER THIS >>>

Who was the person who had the most influence in your life?

It is important to recognize the power of models in our lives. They help us to imagine what is possible. The Holy Family is the best model for us and our family life. "The Christian home is the place where children receive the first proclamation of the faith. For this reason the family home is rightly called 'the domestic church,' a community of grace and prayer, a school of human virtues and of Christian charity" (CCC, 1666).

LET'S TALK >>>

• Have your child name the members of the Holy Family.

• Share a story about how you've honored Mary and/or Joseph.

LET'S PRAY >>>

 Dear Zechariah, Elizabeth, and John, pray for us that God will bless our family with happiness. Amen.

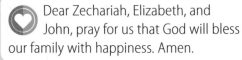 For a multimedia glossary of Catholic Faith Words, Sunday readings, seasonal and Saint resources, and chapter activities go to **aliveinchrist.osv.com**.

About the Bible

 Let Us Pray

Leader: Jesus called God the Father his shepherd. He watches over all of us.

"The LORD is my shepherd; there is nothing I lack." **Psalm 23:1**

All: Help us to trust in you, O God. Amen.

God's Word

Jesus used stories when he spoke to the people. God's promise from long ago came true…"I will open my mouth in parables, I will announce what has lain hidden from the foundation of the world."

Based on Matthew 13:34–35

? What Do You Wonder?

- What are some of the stories that Jesus told?
- Where do you find the stories that Jesus tells us?

Getting Started

In this chapter you will learn about parables, the stories Jesus told to teach others about God's love. You will also learn that the Bible is the Church's holy book that contains stories about God.

In the space below show what you already know about the Bible.

© Our Sunday Visitor

Catholic Faith Words

Here are the vocabulary words for this chapter:

- Old Testament
- New Testament

Write or draw four stories you know from the Bible.

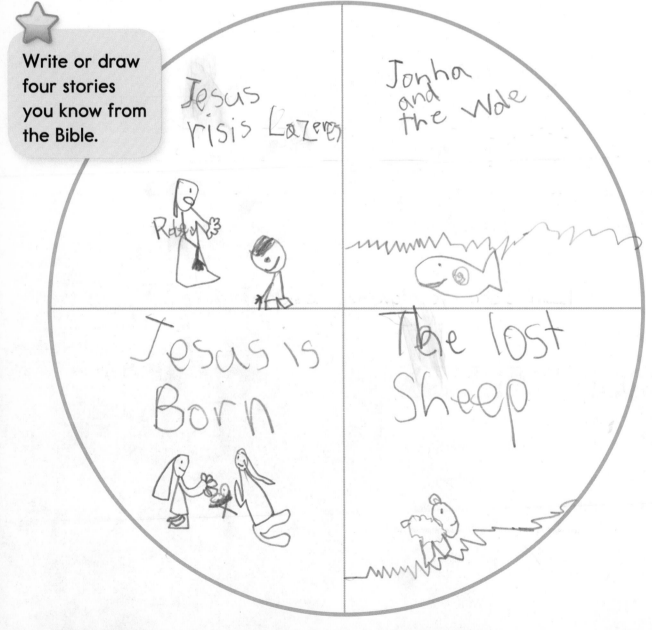

Activity

Reading the Bible Trace the answers about where and how you hear Bible stories.

1. Where do you hear stories from the Bible?

   At home

   At school

2. Who reads the Bible to you?

   My parents

   My teacher

Tell a classmate about your favorite Bible story.

JESUS' MIRACLE

We Learn from Stories

How is God like a shepherd?

Jesus was a wonderful storyteller. His stories tell about God's love. Jesus told this story about a shepherd.

1. Underline what went wrong in the story.

2. Circle what the shepherd did.

 God's Word

The Parable of the Lost Sheep

There was a shepherd. He cared for 100 sheep. One sheep ran away. The shepherd was very worried. The shepherd left all his other sheep. He had to find the sheep that ran away.

The shepherd found the lost sheep. He was very happy. He told all his friends and neighbors that he had found his sheep.

Based on Luke 15:3–6

Our Shepherd

In this story, the shepherd is like God. The sheep are like people. God does not want you to leave him. He will watch over you all the time, just like a shepherd.

When you make bad choices, you are like the lost sheep. Even when you don't choose what is right, God always wants you to come back to him. He wants you to love him and others. He wants you to know that he will always be there for you no matter what.

Activity

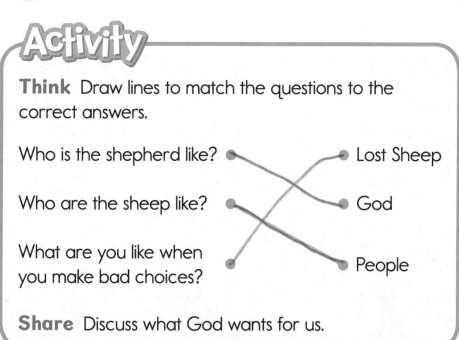

Think Draw lines to match the questions to the correct answers.

Who is the shepherd like?   Lost Sheep

Who are the sheep like?   God

What are you like when you make bad choices?   People

Share Discuss what God wants for us.

Stories about God

What can you find in the Bible?

A parable is a short story that teaches something important. The story you just read about the lost sheep is a parable. Jesus told parables to teach people about God.

Jesus is like a shepherd. He loves all God's people. He always cares for them. Read this parable that Jesus told.

Underline the ways that Jesus is like a shepherd.

 God's Word

The Good Shepherd

"I am the good shepherd, and I know mine and mine know me, just as the Father knows me and I know the Father; and I will lay down my life for the sheep." John 10:14–15

The Holy Book

The parable of the Good Shepherd is in the Bible. The Bible is the Word of God written in human words. The Bible is the Church's holy book.

There are two parts to the Bible. The first part is the **Old Testament**. It is about times before Jesus was born.

The second part is the **New Testament**. It tells about Jesus and his followers. The stories and parables that Jesus told are part of the New Testament.

Catholic Faith Words

Old Testament the first part of the Bible about God and his People before Jesus was born

New Testament the second part of the Bible about the life and teachings of Jesus, his followers, and the early Church

Activity

Write about the Bible Use a Bible to find the answers to these questions.

1. Find the first book in the Old Testament. Trace the name of the book on the line below.

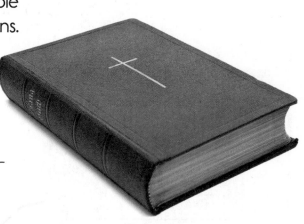

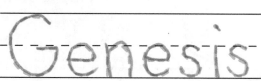

Genesis

2. Find the first book of the New Testament. Trace the name of the book on the line below.

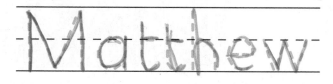

Matthew

Our Catholic Life

What can you find in the Bible?

Our Catholic Tradition

For more, go to page **357**

The Bible is full of stories about God's love. The words of the Bible tell us how to show love for him and others.

You hear stories from the Bible at church, in school, and at home. You may have seen stories from the Bible made into books or videos.

The Two Parts of the Bible

The Old Testament

Here you will find stories about God and his People before Jesus was born. These stories are about holy men and women like Noah, Moses, Ruth, Jonah, and Daniel.

The New Testament

You will find the parables, or teaching stories, Jesus told here. The New Testament also tells about the coming of the Holy Spirit and the work of the first followers of Jesus.

People of Faith

Saint Paul of the Cross, 1694–1775

Saint Paul of the Cross tried being a soldier, but decided that he wanted to be a priest instead. As a young man he spent a lot of time praying and reading the Bible to learn about Jesus. He read about Jesus' Death on the Cross. He wanted to always remember Jesus' sacrifice. That's why he added the words "of the Cross" to his name. Saint Paul helps us to remember that God is close to us and never forgets us.

October 20

Discuss: What story from the Bible helps you remember God's love?

Learn more about Saint Paul at **aliveinchrist.osv.com**

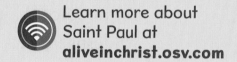

Activity

Follow the Maze Use a pencil or crayon to find the right path through the maze so the shepherd can find his lost sheep.

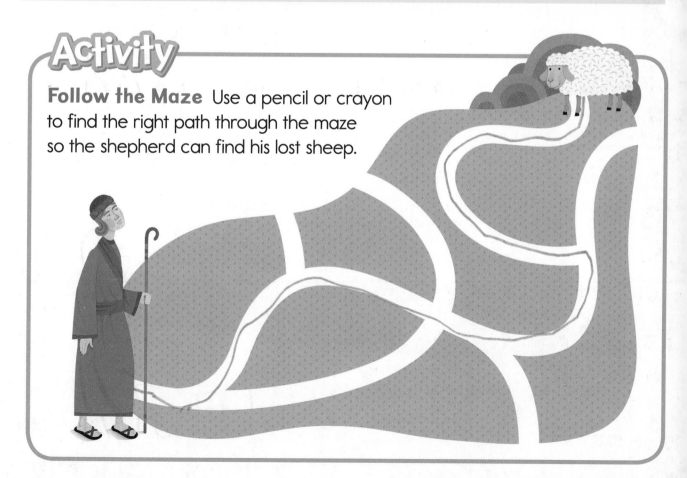

 **Let Us Pray**

Prayer of Thanks

Gather and begin with the Sign of the Cross.

Leader: Thank you, Jesus, for loving us.

All: Thank you, Jesus.

Leader: Thank you, Jesus, for taking care of us.

All: Thank you, Jesus. Amen.

▶ Sing "The Good Shepherd"

Jesus is the Good Shepherd,
he knows his sheep and he loves them.
Jesus is the Good Shepherd;
he loves us all. He loves us all.

Jesus calls our name:

Sing your name twice.

and we come to him running
and running and running
and running and running
and running because we love him.

Chapter 6 Review

A **Work with Words** Circle the correct answer.

1. The _Bible_ is God's Word written in human words.

   (Bible)   prayer

2. The ____ is about Jesus' life and teachings.

   Old Testament   (New Testament)

3. A ____ is a short story that teaches something about God.

   prayer   (parable)

4. The ____ is the first part of the Bible about God and his People before Jesus was born.

   (Old Testament)   New Testament

B **Check Understanding** Draw a heart around the correct answer.

5. How is God like the Good Shepherd?

   He is lost    He loves us

Go to aliveinchrist.osv.com
for an interactive review.

FAMILY+FAITH

LIVING AND LEARNING TOGETHER

YOUR CHILD LEARNED >>>

This chapter teaches about the Bible, the holy book of the Church and its two parts—the Old Testament and the New Testament—that contain stories about God and his love for us.

God's Word

 Read **Matthew 13:10–15** to find out why Jesus used parables to teach.

Catholics Believe

- Jesus told short stories, or parables, to teach others something about God.
- The Bible is the Word of God written in human words.

To learn more, go to the *Catechism of the Catholic Church* #134–139 at **usccb.org**.

People of Faith

This week, your child met Saint Paul of the Cross. He added the words "of the Cross" to his name to remember Jesus' sacrifice.

CHILDREN AT THIS AGE >>>

How They Understand the Parables of Jesus First graders are very concrete thinkers. They learn through their senses and often take things literally. Because of this, they may not grasp the meaning of Jesus' parables, even with explanation. However, familiarity with these important stories Jesus told can lay the foundation for a later, deeper understanding of Jesus' teaching. When your child knows Jesus' parables, it will be easier to teach the great truths they convey when he or she is ready to understand.

CONSIDER THIS >>>

What is your favorite family story?

Stories of our personal history help us to discover that we are part of a bigger picture. Being a member of the Church helps us to be connected to the stories of salvation history. "The Holy Trinity brought the Church into being. The Father called the Church into existence. The Son established the Church. The Holy Spirit filled the Church with power and wisdom at Pentecost. The Holy Trinity abides with the Church always, creatively and providentially" *(USCCA, pp. 112–113).*

LET'S TALK >>>

- Have your child explain what the Bible is.
- Share one of your favorite stories from the Old or New Testaments.

LET'S PRAY >>>

 Dear God, help our family always remember the good things you have done for us and to share those stories with others. Amen.

 For a multimedia glossary of Catholic Faith Words, Sunday readings, seasonal and Saint resources, and chapter activities go to **aliveinchrist.osv.com**.

A **Work with Words** Trace the words to answer the questions.

1. Who are the three Divine Persons in the Holy Trinity?

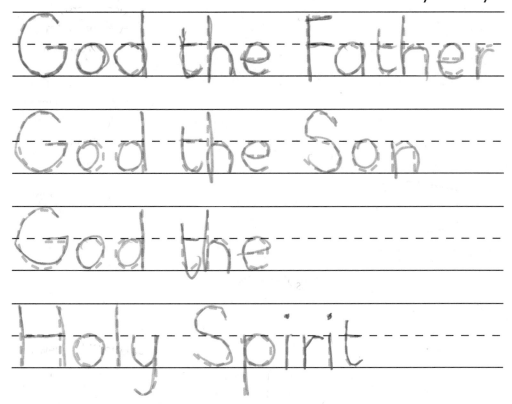

God the Father

God the Son

God the

Holy Spirit

2. Who is the Son of God?

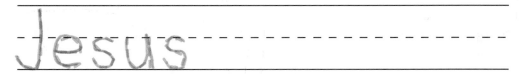

Jesus

3. What can you find in the Bible?

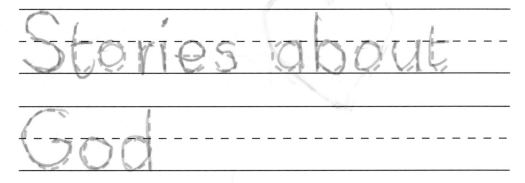

Stories about

God

B **Check Understanding** Circle the correct answer.

4. Jesus taught us to call God by what name?

John   Adam   (Father)

5. Who are Jesus, Mary, and Joseph?

The Trinity   The Church   (The Holy Family)

6. What stories did Jesus tell?

(Parables)   Prayer   Sheep

7. Who made all things?

The Shepherd   (God)   The Family

8. Who did God send to save his people?

(God the Son)   God the Father   Holy Family

9. What is the Church's holy book?

Old Testament   New Testament   (The Bible)

C **Make Connections** Draw one thing that we can learn about God from the Bible.

10.

Jesus Christ

Our Catholic Tradition

- Jesus healed people. When he did this, he showed God's love for them. (CCC, 1509)
- Jesus showed his power when he healed others, and many people believed in him. (CCC, 548)
- Jesus showed us that the most important Commandment is to love God and to love others. (CCC, 2083)
- Jesus showed us how to pray when he taught his friends the Lord's Prayer. (CCC, 2759)

Our Catholic Life

- We can do things to share God's love and help people feel better. (CCC, 1889)
- We show love for God when we pray and read the Bible. We show love for others when we share and listen. (CCC, 1932, 2653)
- In the Lord's Prayer we first praise God the Father then ask for his help. (CCC, 2803)

How does Jesus' command to love God with all your heart lead us to pray and care for others?

Jesus the Healer

 Let Us Pray

Leader: Just as Jesus healed the sick and cared for his followers, the Apostles…

"Know that the LORD works wonders for his faithful one." Psalm 4:4

All: May we have the same faith and trust that Jesus can heal us. Amen.

📖 God's Word

Jesus went to every town and village. He taught in their meeting places and preached the Good News about God's Kingdom. Jesus also healed people with different kinds of disease and sickness. Based on Matthew 9:35

❓ What Do You Wonder?

- How does your faith in Jesus help you?
- When you are sick, what makes you better?

Getting Started

Catholic Faith Words

Here is the vocabulary word for this chapter:

• faith

In this chapter you will learn that Jesus' healings showed God the Father's power and love. You will also learn that our faith helps us believe in all that Jesus said and did.

In the chart below show what you know about how Jesus helped people feel better.

Describe what Jesus is doing in the pictures.

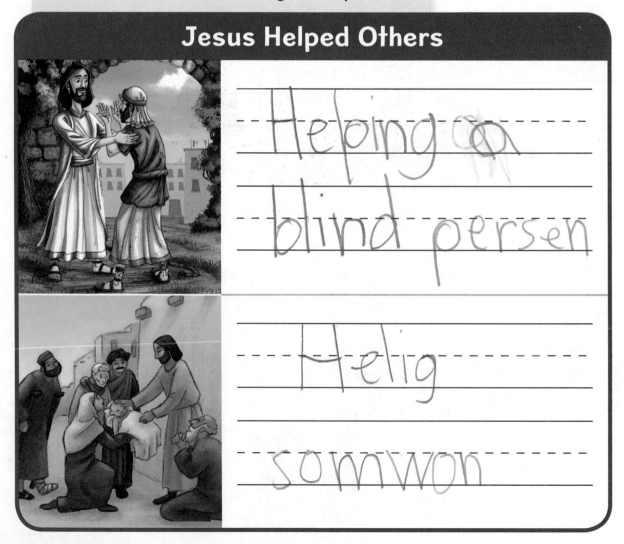

Jesus Helped Others

Helping a blind persen

Helig somwon

A Time You Were Sick Think about a time when you were sick. Who or what made you feel better? Draw or write about it below.

Share God's Love

How did Saint Teresa love people?

As a child, Saint Teresa of Calcutta loved to read stories about missionaries, especially those who spread Jesus' message and cared for people in India. When she became a religious sister she went to India to teach children about God's love.

Known as Mother Teresa, she cared for the poor and sick in India. Read about how she showed God's love.

Before she became a religious sister, Saint Teresa of Calcutta's given name was Agnes.

Saint Teresa of Calcutta

The streets of Calcutta, India, were very crowded with people. Many people were sick. They lived on the streets.

Saint Teresa saw a sick man. His clothes were dirty. He was covered with mud and very thin. The man was dying.

Saint Teresa smiled at him. No one ever smiled at him. She and another religious sister took him to their hospital.

Saint Teresa had a hospital for the dying. There she and other women cared for people who were very sick. They held hands with dying people. They prayed with them and for them.

Circle one thing that Saint Teresa of Calcutta did for those who were sick and dying.

God's Goodness

Saint Teresa of Calcutta knew that God's goodness is in all people. The people she helped could hear love in her voice. They could see love in her sweet smile. They could feel God's love in her touch.

Think Circle the things you can do to help others who are sick.

Share Choose one thing and talk about it with a classmate.

Jesus Heals

Why did Jesus heal people?

When Jesus saw sick people, he felt sad for them. He did whatever he could to help people who needed him.

Catholic

Catholic Faith Words

faith believing in God and all that he helps us understand about himself. Faith leads us to obey God.

Underline what Jesus said to Jairus.

 God's Word

Have Faith

One day a man named Jairus came to Jesus. Jairus said, "My daughter is very sick. I know you can help her."

Jesus agreed. On the way to Jairus's house, a servant came. "It is too late, he said to Jairus. Your daughter is dead."

Jesus told Jairus, "Do not be afraid; just have faith and she will be saved."

Then Jesus went into the house and took the daughter's hand. Jesus said, "Child, arise!" The girl's breath returned, and she got up. Her parents were full of joy.

Based on Luke 8:40–56

Jesus' Healing Actions

Jesus made people well. When Jesus healed people, it was a sign of God's power and love. His healing actions often changed their hearts, too. They saw God's love and power in Jesus. They came to believe in Jesus and have **faith** in him.

Our Catholic Tradition

For more, go to page 380

➤ **What was Jesus' healing a sign of?**

Activity

Draw the Story Draw the part of the story about Jesus' healing that you like best.

Our Catholic Life

How can you help people feel better?

Jesus helped people who were sick. He gave hope and friendship to people who were lonely. He did these things as signs of God's love. You can share signs of God's love, too.

Ways to Help Others

Place a check mark next to things you have done to help someone feel better.

- [ ] Write a note or make a card that says you are thinking of the person.

- [ ] Tell some jokes to cheer up the person.

- [ ] Do a chore to help the person.

- [ ] Pray for the person.

- [ ] Draw a colorful picture for the person.

- [ ] Record a song for the person.

- [ ] Help make a treat for the person to eat when he or she feels better.

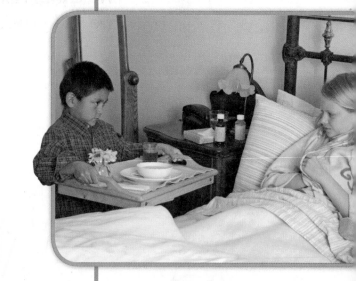

People of Faith

Saint Louise de Marillac, 1591–1660

Saint Louise lived in France. After her husband died, she was very sad. She met Saint Vincent de Paul and they started the Daughters of Charity, a group of religious sisters who worked in hospitals, homes, prisons, and during wars. Saint Louise wanted to share God's love by helping the poor and the sick. There are still over 25,000 Daughters of Charity who help the poor.

March 15

Discuss: How do you share God's love with others?

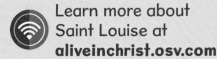 Learn more about Saint Louise at **aliveinchrist.osv.com**

Activity

Thank Someone who has made you feel better when you were sick. Write their name and circle the thing that they gave you to help you feel better.

_____

Dear -

_____

Thank you for giving me:

Food

Love

Medicine

 **Let Us Pray**

Prayer for Healing

Gather and begin with the Sign of the Cross.

Leader: Jesus, Son of God, we pray for those who are sick. For children who are sick, we pray.

All: Help them be strong and well again.

Leader: Jesus, Son of God, we pray for those who are sick. For children who are sick, we pray.

All: Help them be strong and well again.

Leader: For all people who are sick, we pray.

All: Help them be strong and well again.

Leader: Jesus, Son of God, we pray for those who take care of the sick. For all who care for others, we pray.

All: Give them grace and strength. Amen.

Sing "Heal Us, Lord"
Heal us, Lord.
We feel the power of
your love.
Let your Spirit
come unto us.
© 2001, John Burland.
All rights reserved.

Chapter 7 Review

A **Check Understanding** Trace the words to answer the questions.

1. What is faith?

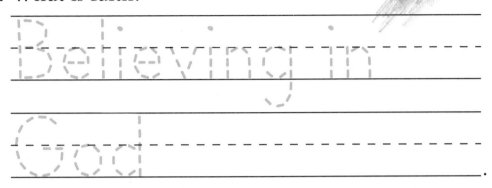

Believing in God.

2. What did Jesus do to show God's power and love?

He healed.

3. What did Blessed Mother Teresa of Calcutta do to show God's love to sick people?

She cured.

B **Make Connections** Circle the right answer.

4. How can you help a sick person?

   play   fight   pray

5. How can you help a sad person?

   swim   visit them   sleep

Go to aliveinchrist.osv.com
for an interactive review.

FAMILY+FAITH
LIVING AND LEARNING TOGETHER

YOUR CHILD LEARNED >>>

This chapter is about how Jesus healed people who were sick and cared for those who were lonely; he asks us to help others who are sick or sad.

God's Word

 Read **Matthew 9** to learn about Jesus' teachings and the many miracles that he worked.

Catholics Believe

• Jesus' healing actions show God's power and love.

• Faith is the gift of believing in God and doing as he asks.

To learn more, go to the *Catechism of the Catholic Church* #547–550 at **usccb.org**.

People of Faith

This week, your child met Saint Louise de Marillac, the founder of a religious order dedicated to the care of those who are poor and sick.

CHILDREN AT THIS AGE >>>

How They Understand Jesus' Healings Illnesses and healing are still mysterious processes for many first grade children. As adults, we understand Jesus' healings as being miraculous (a sign of his power and his spiritual strength), but your child might sometimes see the healing and care that parents and doctors give as being quite similar. One difference we can point out is the immediacy of healing in Jesus' ministry. This shows that Jesus was able to heal in a way that no one else could.

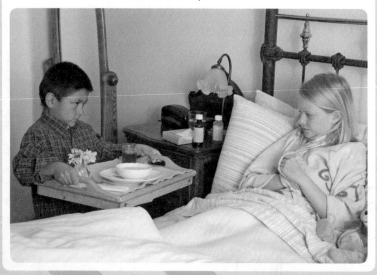

CONSIDER THIS >>>

What makes a relationship grow?

Relationships require a commitment of time and presence. Faith is a relationship with God that begins as a gift, but like all our relationships requires time and presence. "God never forces his truth and love upon us. He reveals himself to us as free human beings, and our faith response to him is made within the context of our freedom" (*USCCA*, p. 39).

LET'S TALK >>>

• Ask your child how Jesus cared for those who were sick.

• Share a time when someone made you feel better physically, emotionally, or spiritually.

LET'S PRAY >>>

Dear Saint Louise, pray for us so we can be patient when we are sick and help us be kind to those who are feeling sad. Amen.

 For a multimedia glossary of Catholic Faith Words, Sunday readings, seasonal and Saint resources, and chapter activities go to **aliveinchrist.osv.com**.

Jesus Teaches Love

 Let Us Pray

Leader: God, we want to follow your teachings.

"I will keep your law always,
    for all time and forever."   Psalm 119:44

All: God, we want to follow your teachings.
Amen.

📖 God's Word

One of the men asked Jesus: "Teacher, what is the most important commandment?" Jesus answered: "Love the Lord your God with all your heart, soul, and mind...and love others as much as you love yourself."   Based on Mark 12:28–31

? What Do You Wonder?

- Why is it important to love others?
- How do you show love?

Getting Started

In this chapter you will learn that a Commandment is a law that God made. You will also learn that God wants us to love him most of all and to love other people.

Use the boxes below to show who or what reminds you of God's love.

Draw four people, places, or things that show or remind you of God's love.

God's Love

Catholic Faith Words

Here are the vocabulary words for this chapter:

- Commandment

- Great Commandment

Activity

Special Word Color the 1's red, the 2's blue, the 3's yellow, the 4's green, and the 5's purple to discover a special word.

As a class, talk about the different ways children your age show love.

Show Your Love

What gift can you give?

The Gift

Brooke asked, "Mom, what can I do for Grandpa's birthday?"

Mom said, "Let's think. What do you and Grandpa like to do?"

"We like to build sandcastles at the beach. He plays checkers with me, too," said Brooke.

Mom asked, "Is there anything else?"

"Yes!" Brooke said. "He likes my drawings. He always saves them. I've got it! Thanks, Mom!"

Underline the things that Brooke and her Grandpa like.

On Grandpa's birthday, Brooke gave him a gift.

It was a drawing of Brooke and Grandpa playing checkers together. The picture said, "I love you, Grandpa."

"Thank you, Brooke," said Grandpa. "This is the best gift! I will hang it up for everyone to see."

"Great!" Brooke said happily. "Let's go play checkers!"

Activity

Think How did Brooke show love with her gift? Draw one way you can show love to someone else.

Share your work with a classmate.

Love God and Others

What did Jesus teach about love?

Our Catholic Tradition

For more, go to page 357

Brooke's drawing was a sign of her love for her Grandpa. Listen to one of Jesus' teachings on love.

Circle what the law says about loving God and others.

 God's Word

The Greatest Commandment

One day a man said, "I want to be happy with God forever. What should I do?"

Jesus asked, "What is written in the law?"

The man replied, "You shall love the Lord, your God, with all your heart, with all your being, with all your strength, and with all your mind, and your neighbor as yourself."

Jesus said, "You have answered correctly." Based on Luke 10:25–28

The Great Commandment

A **Commandment** is a law that God made for people to obey. Loving God and others is the most important Commandment. This law is called the Great Commandment.

The **Great Commandment** teaches you to love God more than anything. It also tells you to love others as you love yourself.

➡ **What are some ways parents show love to their children?**

Catholic Faith Words

Commandment a law that God made for people to obey

Great Commandment the law that tells you to love God above all else and to love others the way you love yourself

Activity

Match the Picture Match the actions in the pictures to the different ways that someone in your family shows love for God and others.

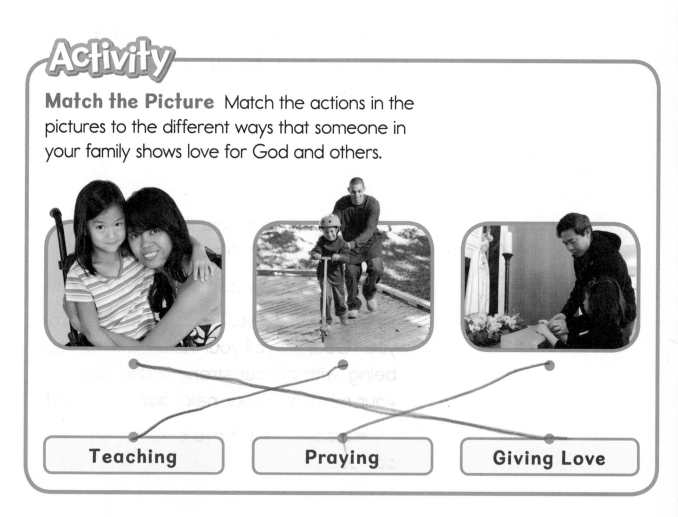

| Teaching | Praying | Giving Love |

© Our Sunday Visitor

Our Catholic Life

How can you show love for God and for others?

There are many ways to keep the Great Commandment. Here are some ways that you can show love for God and for others.

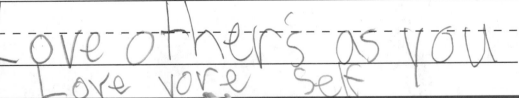

Love God and Others

Love God	Love Others
Pray at meals and bedtime.	Do what parents and family members ask of you without grumbling.
Learn about God at home, at church, and in school.	Share what you have.
Get to know the stories in the Bible.	Be kind. Don't tease or fight.

Love others as you Love yore self

On the line above, write one way you can love God and love others.

© Our Sunday Visitor

People of Faith

Saint Thomas of Villanova, 1486–1555

Saint Thomas was a teacher, a monk, and a bishop in Spain. He wanted to love people like Jesus did. He always tried to live the Great Commandment. Saint Thomas gave his money to people who had nothing. He tried to help them find work, too. He found homes for many orphaned children. He paid to free many slaves. Because of all the good things he did, Saint Thomas was called "Father of the Poor."

September 22

Discuss: When has your family given food to the poor?

 Learn more about Saint Thomas at **aliveinchrist.osv.com**

Activity

Draw a picture of a time when you shared with someone else.

 **Let Us Pray**

Pray with God's Word

Gather and begin with the Sign of the Cross.

Leader: Blessed be God.

All: Blessed be God forever.

Leader: A reading from the holy Gospel according to Matthew.

Read Matthew 5:14–16.

The Gospel of the Lord.

All: Praise to you, Lord Jesus Christ.

 Sing "Loving God"

Love the Lord, your God,
with all your heart,
with all your soul,
with all your mind,
and with all your strength.

Love the Lord, your God,
with all your heart,
with all your soul,
with all your mind,
and with all your strength.

Chapter 8 Review

© Our Sunday Visitor

A **Work with Words** Circle the correct word to complete each sentence.

1. A Commandment is a ____ God made for people to obey.

parable   (law)

2. ____ taught the Great Commandment.

(Jesus)   Jairus

3. The Great Commandment begins with ____ God.

(loving)   knowing

4. You can love God by ____.

(praying)   pushing

B **Check Understanding** Draw a picture to show a way to love others.

5.

 Go to **aliveinchrist.osv.com** for an interactive review.

FAMILY+FAITH
LIVING AND LEARNING TOGETHER

YOUR CHILD LEARNED >>>

This chapter explains that a Commandment is a law God made for people to obey, and that we are called to love God and others.

God's Word

 Read **Mark 12:28–31** to learn more about how Jesus wants us to love God.

Catholics Believe

- A Commandment is a law that God made for people to obey.
- The Great Commandment teaches that you are to love God above all else and love others as you love yourself.

To learn more, go to the *Catechism of the Catholic Church* #2052–2055 at **usccb.org**.

People of Faith

This week, your child met Saint Thomas of Villanova, a Spanish bishop whose generosity to the poor gave him the name, "Father of the Poor."

CHILDREN AT THIS AGE >>>

How They Understand the Great Commandment The concrete way of thinking that is characteristic of most first graders may sometimes make it difficult for them to know how to love God, whom they cannot see, above all things. However, you can make this practical for your child by helping him or her understand that we show our love for God by talking with him and making the good choices he wants us to make. We also show love to God when we are kind and loving toward others.

CONSIDER THIS >>>

What is the greatest priority in your life?

Our first response would probably be family. Yet, Jesus said we must love God first then everything falls in order, including our relationships. "You shall love the Lord, your God, with all your heart, with all your soul, and with all your mind. This is the greatest and the first commandment. The second is like it: You shall love your neighbor as yourself" (**Matthew 22:37–39**).

LET'S TALK >>>

- Have your child name one way he/she shows love to God and one way he/she shows love to others.
- Talk about why God's laws are important.

LET'S PRAY >>>

 Saint Thomas, help us care for people who don't have enough money and people who are hungry. Amen.

 For a multimedia glossary of Catholic Faith Words, Sunday readings, seasonal and Saint resources, and chapter activities go to **aliveinchrist.osv.com**.

Jesus Teaches Us to Pray

 Let Us Pray

Leader: God, we praise you always.

"Every day I will bless you;
   I will praise your name forever and
   ever." Psalm 145:2

All: God, we praise you always. Amen.

God's Word

When you pray, go into a room alone and close the door. Pray to God in private. God knows what you are doing and will reward you. When you pray, you don't have to talk on and on. God will listen to your short and long prayers. God knows what you need before you ask. Based on Matthew 6:6–8

? What Do You Wonder?

- Did Jesus pray?
- Why do we sometimes pray alone and sometimes together?

Getting Started

Catholic Faith Words

Here are the vocabulary words for this chapter:

- prayer
- Lord's Prayer

In this chapter you will learn that we pray by talking or listening to God. You will also learn how Jesus taught us a prayer called the Lord's Prayer.

Use the table below to show which prayers you already know.

 Check off the prayers that you know and answer the question.

Prayers I Know

✓ The Sign of the Cross	✓ The Lord's Prayer
✓ The Hail Mary	✓ The Glory Be
✓ The Guardian Angel Prayer	☐ The Apostles' Creed

What are some words you know from a prayer you've heard before?

Our Father.

Hail Mary.

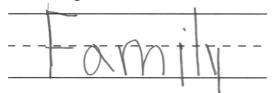

Activity

Praying to God Answer the questions about what you say when you pray.

1. What is one thing you thank God for at night?

Family

Teachers

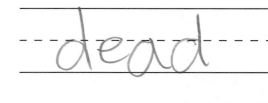

2. Who do you pray for?

dead

3. What can you tell God about your day?

wonderful

Stay Close to God

What are some ways to pray?

© Our Sunday Visitor

Talking with family and friends helps you feel close to them. Talking to and listening to God is called **prayer**.

God wants us to be his friends. He asks us to pray to him. We feel close to God when we pray.

Blessing prayers thank God for the good things he gives you. They ask God to keep caring for you and others.

➡ **What are some things you can thank God for when you pray?**

Catholic Faith Words

prayer talking to and listening to God

Underline what it means to pray.

Pray Anywhere

You can pray wherever you are. You can talk to God at home or in church. You can pray in your classroom or on the playground.

Begin your prayer by thanking God the Father for all that he gives you.

Wherever you are, God will hear you. You can say your own prayer. You can say prayers of the Church. You can pray silently or out loud. Praying with your family before meals and at bedtime is a special way to stay close to God and one another.

Activity

Think Draw a picture of something you want to thank God for.

Share your picture with a classmate.

Taking care of me.

Learn to Pray

What special prayer did Jesus give his followers?

Our Catholic Tradition
For more, go to page **381**

You can learn songs, words, and actions to talk with God. You can use them to pray any time you wish.

The Church family can learn to pray together from the Bible. We should always give thanks to God for all he has given us. Let's read what Saint Paul tells us are some ways we can do that:

1. Circle ways that we can give thanks to God.

2. Color in the music notes below.

 God's Word

How to Pray

Be filled with the Holy Spirit. Sing psalms, hymns, and spiritual songs—singing and playing to the Lord in your hearts, giving thanks always and for everything in the name of our Lord Jesus Christ to God the Father.   **Based on Ephesians 5:18–20**

The Lord's Prayer

At Mass and at other times, you pray a very important prayer called the **Lord's Prayer**. Jesus taught his friends to pray this way.

The Lord's Prayer

Our Father, who art in heaven,
hallowed be thy name;
thy kingdom come,
thy will be done
on earth as it is in heaven.
Give us this day our daily bread,
and forgive us our trespasses,
as we forgive those who
    trespass against us;
and lead us not into temptation,
but deliver us from evil. Amen.

Catholic Faith Words

Lord's Prayer the prayer Jesus taught his followers to pray to God the Father. This prayer is also called the Our Father.

Activity

Pray Together Write the name of someone that you pray with.

Amelias Adam and Dad

Our Catholic Life

What do we ask God when we pray the Lord's Prayer?

The chart below explains what we are praising and asking God for when we pray the Lord's Prayer.

The Lord's Prayer

Words of the Prayer	What They Mean
Our Father, who art in heaven, hallowed be thy name;	God our Father, may we praise your holy name.
Thy kingdom come, thy will be done on earth as it is in heaven.	May we do what you ask here on Earth as the angels and Saints do in Heaven.
Give us this day our daily bread,	May we have the things we need today.
and forgive us our trespasses, as we forgive those who trespass against us;	Please forgive us for the things we do wrong, and help us forgive those who hurt us.
and lead us not into temptation, but deliver us from evil.	Keep us safe from anything that would harm us or lead us away from you.
Amen!	May it be so!

People of Faith

Saint Ephrem the Hymnist, 306–373

Saint Ephrem was a teacher and a poet, but he is best known for writing hymns. He wrote more than 400 hymns! He used the popular songs of his time, but changed the words to help people learn about Jesus and Mary and praise God. His hymns remind us how much God loves us and wants us to love him.

June 9

Discuss: How do you tell others how much God loves you?

Learn more about Saint Ephrem at **aliveinchrist.osv.com**

Activity

Trace the Words Trace the words to complete the first lines of the Lord's Prayer.

Our Father,

who art in heaven,

hallowed be thy name.

Anytime Prayer

Gather and begin with the
Sign of the Cross.

Leader: We can pray in the morning,
at the start of each day.

All: We can pray in the morning, at the start
of each day.

Leader: And at every mealtime, we bow heads
and pray.

All: And at every mealtime, we bow heads
and pray.

Leader: We pray at our bedtime, at the end of
our days.

All: We pray at our bedtime, at the end of
our days.

Leader: For God is our Father, who listens always.

All: For God is our Father, who listens always.

Leader: Let us join in prayer to God our Father.

Pray the Lord's Prayer together.

All: Sing "The Lord's Prayer"

A **Work with Words** Trace the words to complete the sentence.

1. You can pray by 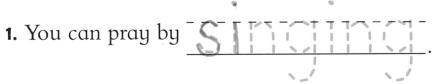.

2. One name to call God when you pray is
.

3. Jesus taught his friends to pray the
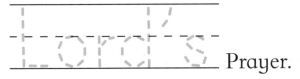 Prayer.

4. 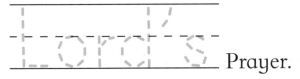 is talking and listening

to God.

B **Check Understanding** Circle the correct answers.

5. What pictures show ways to pray?

Singing to God   **Talking to God**   **Swimming**

Go to **aliveinchrist.osv.com**
for an interactive review.

© Our Sunday Visitor

YOUR CHILD LEARNED >>>

The chapter describes the ways and reasons we pray and introduces the words and meaning of the Lord's Prayer.

God's Word

 Read **Matthew 6:6–8** to learn the ways that Jesus says we can pray.

Catholics Believe

- Prayer is talking and listening to God.
- Jesus taught his friends how to pray the Lord's Prayer.

To learn more, go to the *Catechism of the Catholic Church* #2607–2612 at **usccb.org**.

People of Faith

This week, your child met Saint Ephrem. He loved to sing and give praise to God. He personally wrote more than 400 hymns.

CHILDREN AT THIS AGE >>>

How They Understand Prayer Children who grow up in Catholic families, parishes, and schools have many opportunities to see people praying and to say prayers in groups. Children begin to respond to and relate to an unseen God when they see adults in their lives talking to God. It's important for your child to know that God is a friend he or she can talk to in his or her own words. It's also important to teach your child that prayer is listening as well as speaking.

CONSIDER THIS >>>

Who did you most depend on as a child?

Many people might answer a parent, or family member. It is necessary for a child's emotional well-being to know that there is someone he/she can depend upon, someone who is trustworthy. "A term that our Lord uses for Father is *'Abba!'* [Daddy] This implies that Jesus is saying that a relationship with God [the Father] should be like that of a child, very close, personal, and dependent" (*USCCA, p. 484*).

LET'S TALK >>>

- Talk with your child about the different ways your family prays together.
- Describe your favorite time or place to pray.

LET'S PRAY >>>

 Dear God, help us to know how much you love us and let us always sing to you like Saint Ephrem did. Amen.

 For a multimedia glossary of Catholic Faith Words, Sunday readings, seasonal and Saint resources, and chapter activities go to **aliveinchrist.osv.com**.

A **Work with Words** Circle the correct answer.

1. ____ is talking to and listening to God.

   Playing   Prayer

2. A ____ is a law God made for people to obey.

   Commandment   parable

3. ____ is the gift of believing in God and doing as he asks.

   Love   Faith

4. The Great Commandment is about ____ God above all else and your neighbor as yourself.

   knowing   loving

5. ____ teaches you to love God and others.

   Jesus   Jairus

B **Check Understanding** Draw a line from the phrase in Column A to the correct word or words in Column B.

Column A	Column B
6. What Jesus did for some sick people	love
7. What God wants to be	healed
8. A gift you can give	your friend
9. Where you can pray	prayers
10. God hears your	everywhere

Circle the words in the word search.

11–13.

Word Bank

Love

Pray

Laws

```
L  A  W  S  P  C
K  U  U  V  R  V
B  L  F  W  A  A
V  O  A  L  Y  L
Q  V  T  L  I  L
P  E  D  Z  M  D
```

C **Make Connections** Trace the words to answer the questions.

14. What prayer did Jesus teach?

The Lord's
Prayer

15. How did Mother Teresa show God's love to others?

She cared for
people who
were sick.

The Church

Our Catholic Tradition

- The Church is made up of the baptized people who believe in God and follow Jesus. (CCC, 751–752)

- We say "yes" to Jesus and as his Church share his message of God's Kingdom. (CCC, 763)

- God the Holy Spirit is at work with God the Father and God the Son in the whole world. (CCC, 686)

- The Holy Spirit guides people in the Church to live holy lives like the Saints. (CCC, 736)

Our Catholic Life

- With faith and obedience, Mary said "yes" to God, and became the Mother of his Son. (CCC, 506, 511)

- The Gifts of the Holy Spirit help us follow his guidance and live as Jesus' friends. (CCC, 1830)

- The Holy Spirit is with us every day and helps us live like the Saints. (CCC, 738)

How does the Holy Spirit help us to live as holy people?

Notre Dame Cathedral Paris, France

Responding to God

 Let Us Pray

Leader: God, you are always faithful to us, help us to be faithful to you.

"I will praise you among the peoples, Lord;
I will chant your praise among the nations." Psalm 57:10

All: Dear God, help us to always say "yes" to you. Amen.

 God's Word

"By faith Noah, warned about what was not yet seen, with reverence built an ark for the salvation of his household…he…[Noah] inherited the righteousness that comes through faith." Hebrews 11:7

 **What Do You Wonder?**

- What does faithful mean?
- How does God speak to us today?

Getting Started

In this chapter you will learn that everyone is invited into God's Kingdom. The Church is the community of baptized people who believe in God and follow Jesus.

Use the boxes below to show some places you have been invited.

Write the names of four places you have been invited to.

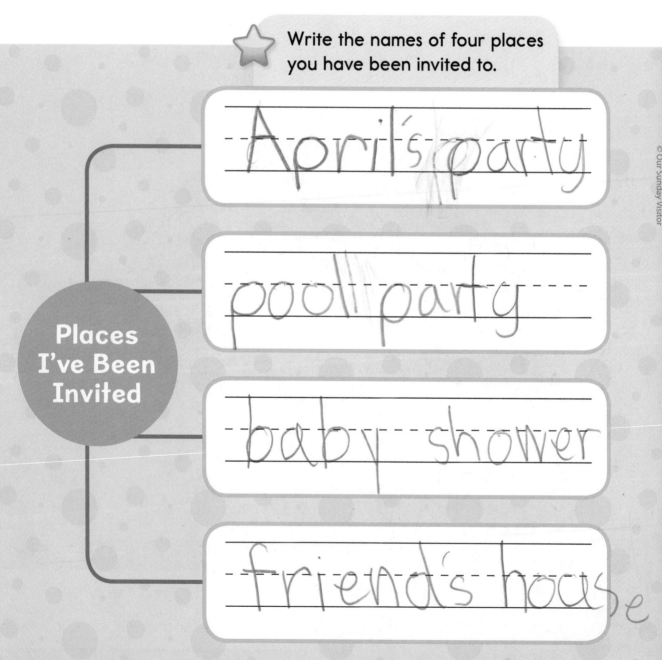

Places I've Been Invited

April's party

pool party

baby shower

friend's house

Catholic **Faith Words**

Here are the vocabulary words for this chapter:

- Kingdom of God
- Church

Activity

Rainbows We often get excited when we see a rainbow. In science we learn that light and water make a rainbow. In this chapter we will learn how God uses the rainbow. Color the rainbow and imagine how God will use it.

Trust in God

What did God promise Noah?

The story of Noah is in the Old Testament. Noah said "yes" when God asked him a very big question.

🔵 God's Word

Noah Says "Yes"

Noah was a good man. God told Noah to build an ark, or very large boat.

God said it was going to rain for forty days and forty nights. There would be a flood. God wanted Noah to be safe.

⭐ Underline what God told Noah to do.

Noah said "Yes, I will!" He built the ark even though he saw no rain anywhere.

God told Noah to take his family and two of each kind of animal into the ark. Noah said, "Yes!" and did as God said.

Then the rains came. The rivers swelled until they flooded all the Earth. Noah, his family, and all the animals stayed dry in the ark.

After forty days, the rain stopped. God promised that water would never flood the whole Earth again.

God gave Noah and his family a sign of his promise. God put a rainbow in the sky.

Based on Genesis 6:14–22, 7:1–10, 9:17

Activity

Think How do you think Noah felt when he saw God's rainbow?

joyful

Share Talk with a classmate about God's promise.

All Are Invited

How do you say "yes" to God?

Jesus told a story about God's care for all people. In the story, everyone is invited into the **Kingdom of God**, the world of love, peace, and justice in Heaven that is still being built on Earth.

Underline what the rich man said when no one showed up for the party.

 **God's Word**

The Parable of the Great Feast

A rich man gave a big party. He invited many people. No one came.

The rich man spoke to his servants. "Go out and invite those who are poor, blind, and lame."

The servants did as the man asked. Soon the house was filled with happy people. There still was room for more people.

The rich man said, "Go and find people anywhere you can. Ask them to come to my party." Based on Luke 14:16–23

The Church

The **Church** shares Jesus' message about God's Kingdom.

You became a member of the Church when you were baptized. Your parents said "yes" to God for you. Now you can say "yes" to God for yourself.

You share love as a member of the Church. You work together with God as he builds his Kingdom.

You can invite others into God's Kingdom. You can ask them to say "yes" to God, too.

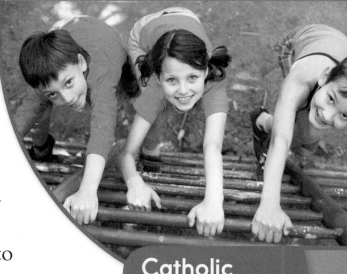

Catholic Faith Words

Kingdom of God the world of love, peace, and justice that is in Heaven and is still being built on Earth

Church the community of all baptized people who believe in God and follow Jesus

Activity

Find the Hidden Word
Color the X's red and the O's blue, green, or yellow to find what you say when God calls you into his Kingdom.

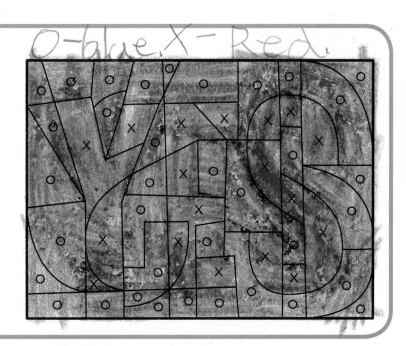

Our Catholic Life

How did Mary answer God's question?

Our Catholic Tradition
For more, go to page 362

God asked Mary to do something special, just as he had asked Noah. Here is Mary's story.

Mary Says "Yes"

Key

🙏 angel   👰 Mary   👶 baby   ❓ question

One day 👰 was praying. An 🙏 came to see her.

The 🙏 was God's messenger. The 🙏 told 👰 that

God had a ❓ for her.

He wanted 👰 to have a 👶. This 👶 would be very

special. This 👶 would be God's Son. 👰 loved God very

much. The 🙏 asked 👰 what he should tell God. And

👰 said, "Tell God yes!"

People of Faith

© Our Sunday Visitor

Blessed Mary Theresa of Jesus Gerhardinger, 1797–1879

Caroline Gerhardinger was born in Germany. She was a teacher, but she believed Jesus was asking her to be a religious sister. She always said "yes" to Jesus, so she started the School Sisters of Notre Dame. Caroline's new name was Mary Theresa of Jesus. She opened schools in Germany and the United States. She was happy to do what Jesus asked.

May 9

Discuss: Name one thing Jesus is asking you to do.

 Learn more about Blessed Mary Theresa at **aliveinchrist.osv.com**

Activity

Draw a scene from the story of Mary saying "yes" to God.

191

 **Let Us Pray**

"Yes" Prayer

Gather and begin with the Sign of the Cross.

Leader: Lord, you ask us to be kind to our families.

All: We say "yes!"

Leader: You ask us to share what we have.

All: We say "yes!"

Leader: You want us to ask everyone to play.

All: We say "yes!"

Leader: Let us pray.

Bow your heads as the leader prays.

All: Amen.

 Sing "Saying Yes"

Saying yes, saying yes to our God.
Jesus, you're my friend.
You are here with me.
I know you are always
by my side.

Chapter 10 Review

A **Work with Words** Circle the correct word to complete each sentence.

1. Mary said _yes_ to God's invitation.

   "yes" *(circled)*   **"no"**

2. God invites _all_ people into his Kingdom.

   all *(circled)*   **some**

3. Being _kind_ is a way of saying "yes" to God.

   kind   **unfair**

4. The community of baptized people who believe in God and follow Jesus is called _the class_.

   the Church   **the class** *(circled)*

5. God put a _rainbow_ in the sky as a sign to Noah.

   bird   **rainbow** *(circled)*

B **Check Understanding** Mark an X in front of the ways to say "yes" to God.

6. ☒ Pray with your family.

7. ☒ Take care of a brother or sister.

8. no! Argue with your parents.

Go to aliveinchrist.osv.com for an interactive review.

© Our Sunday Visitor

FAMILY+FAITH
LIVING AND LEARNING TOGETHER

YOUR CHILD LEARNED >>>

This chapter examines the story of Noah and how Catholics say "yes" to God and describes the Kingdom of God as the world of love, peace, and justice that is in Heaven and is still being built on Earth.

God's Word

 Read **Hebrews 11:7** to learn why Noah was given the blessings that come to those who believe.

Catholics Believe

- God invites everyone into his Kingdom.
- The Church is the community of all baptized people who believe in God and follow Jesus.

To learn more, go to the *Catechism of the Catholic Church* #541–546 at **usccb.org**.

People of Faith

This week, your child met Blessed Mary Theresa of Jesus, the founder of the School Sisters of Notre Dame.

CHILDREN AT THIS AGE >>>

How They Understand Saying "Yes" to God God speaks to us in many ways. We simply need to learn to listen to his voice. Before first-graders can understand what it means to say "yes" to God, they must understand how to recognize the call of God. They can do this when adults in their lives help them to hear God's Word in Scripture. Children also experience God's call in their talents, dreams, and opportunities in their daily lives. As time goes on, your child will become better and better at answering the question, "What might God be saying to me right now?"

CONSIDER THIS >>>

When did you realize that your perspective was limited by your personal experience?

You may have realized this when you got married and your spouse's family did things differently, or when you went to a foreign country, or made a friend from another place in the world. As human beings we are limited. We need God's help to recognize what is truth. "…the Holy Spirit, dwelling in the Church, draws the whole body of the faithful to believe what truly belongs to the faith" (*USCCA, 25*).

LET'S TALK >>>

- Talk about the teacher who first taught you about God.
- Give an example of a time in your life when you've said "yes" to God.

LET'S PRAY >>>

 Dear God, help us appreciate our parish workers and teachers. Thank you for the love they show. Amen.

For a multimedia glossary of Catholic Faith Words, Sunday readings, seasonal and Saint resources, and chapter activities go to **aliveinchrist.osv.com**.

The Church's Guide

 Let Us Pray

Leader: Thank you, God, for your Holy Spirit.

"Teach me to do your will,
for you are my God.
May your kind spirit guide me
on ground that is level." Psalm 143:10

All: Holy Spirit, guide and teach us. Amen.

① God's Word

"…the fruit of the Spirit is love, joy, peace, patience, kindness, generosity, faithfulness, gentleness, self-control.…If we live in the Spirit, let us also follow the Spirit."
Galatians 5:22–23, 25

? What Do You Wonder?

- What helps you be patient and kind, to show love?
- How do you know that the Holy Spirit is with you?

Getting Started

Catholic Faith Words

Here is the vocabulary word for this chapter:

- Holy Spirit

In this chapter you will learn that the Holy Spirit is the Third Divine Person of the Holy Trinity. You will also learn that the Holy Spirit fills our hearts with love and guides the Church.

Use the chart below to show what you know about people who guide us.

Name the type of guides shown in the pictures.

People Who Guide Us

Tourguied

priest

coach

Special Guide Write the name of someone who guides you and teaches you.

Angla my Angel

Draw one way this person guides you.

Guides are there to help us on our journey.

God the Holy Spirit

How does the Holy Spirit guide us?

We need guides to help lead us and teach us. A ranger guides people who visit a park. A tour guide helps people to find important places in a city that they are visiting. A guide in the children's museum can help children to learn about the interesting things that are there.

You need a guide to stay close to God the Father and to Jesus, who is also God the Son. God the **Holy Spirit** will help guide you.

The Work of the Holy Spirit

Jesus would soon be going back to God the Father. He promised his followers that a helper would come.

 God's Word

Jesus Promises the Holy Spirit

Jesus said, "The holy Spirit that the Father will send in my name—he will teach you everything and remind you of all that [I] told you." John 14:26

Our Catholic Tradition
For more, go to page **360**

The guide who came to them is the Holy Spirit. The Holy Spirit is with us today. He lives in the whole Church.

Underline the guide that Jesus promised to send.

Activity

Think How is the Holy Spirit a guide to the whole Church? Connect the dots to find a symbol of the Holy Spirit.

Share Talk about how the Holy Spirit is a guide.

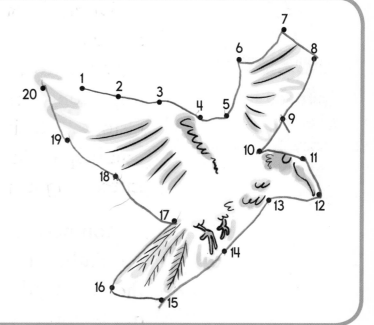

Ways to God

Who can show you the way to God?

Sometimes other people can show us the way to God. Saint Thérèse found a simple way to God.

Saint Thérèse of Lisieux

Thérèse was the youngest child in her family. She knew that God loved her. She loved God very much, too.

She felt that God had not called her to do some of the great big, brave things that some of the Saints had done. But she knew she could still work for God through her little jobs. This is called "the little way." She knew that God would see the love in her work.

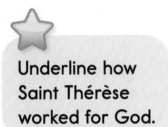
Underline how Saint Thérèse worked for God.

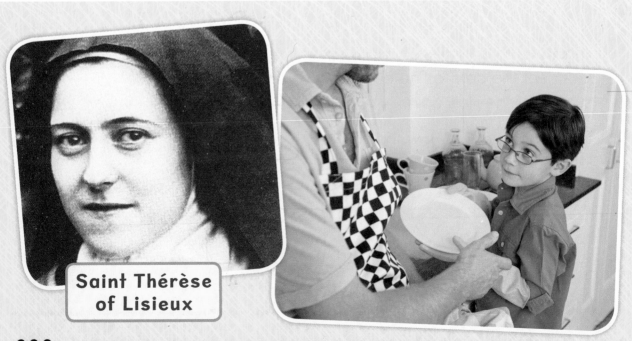
Saint Thérèse of Lisieux

After Thérèse grew up, she wrote about her little way in a book. Many people read the book and followed the little way. Thérèse helped many people find God. She is a special Saint.

→ **How does Saint Thérèse's little way help people do what God asks?**

A Guide for Everyone

Saint Thérèse led people to God's love. She did this because God the Holy Spirit guided her work. The Holy Spirit guides you, too. He will keep you close to God the Father and to God the Son.

Activity

Use the Code Solve the code to learn who guides the Church. Write the letter that matches each number in the phrase below.

1 = H	2 = I	3 = L	4 = O	5 = P
6 = R	7 = S	8 = T	9 = Y	

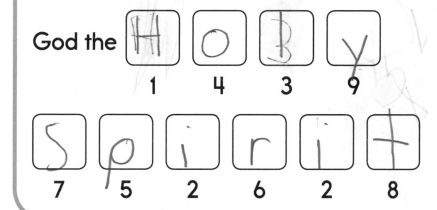

God the

H	O	B	Y
1	4	3	9

S	p	i	r	i	t
7	5	2	6	2	8

Our Catholic Life

How does the Holy Spirit help you?

The Holy Spirit came to help Jesus' friends. He gave them gifts like courage and understanding. Here are the Gifts the Holy Spirit gives you.

Check off two Gifts of the Holy Spirit that you have seen in your family this week.

Gifts of the Holy Spirit

	Gift	How it Helps
✓	wisdom	helps you see yourself and others as God sees you
✓	understanding	helps you get along with others
✓	right judgment (counsel)	helps you make good choices
✓	courage (fortitude)	helps you act bravely
✓	knowledge	helps you know God better
✓	reverence (piety)	helps you pray every day
✓	wonder and awe (fear of the Lord)	helps you understand how great and powerful God is

People of Faith

Saint Rose of Lima, 1586–1617

Saint Rose of Lima was named Isabel at birth. Her family said she was as pretty as a flower, so they called her "Rose." The Holy Spirit gave Rose the gift of piety. She prayed and fasted every day. She loved God's wonderful world. She used her gift to grow beautiful flowers that she sold to help support her family and care for the poor.

August 23

Discuss: What gifts has the Holy Spirit given you?

Learn more about Saint Rose of Lima at **aliveinchrist.osv.com**

Activity

Follow the Holy Spirit If the action below shows love for God and others, color the dove of the Spirit. If the action does not show love, cross out the dove.

 Share your new toy with a friend.

 Call someone a bad name.

 Help fold the laundry.

 Pray.

 Throw trash on the playground.

 **Let Us Pray**

Asking Prayer

Gather and begin with the Sign of the Cross.

Leader: When I ask others to play,

All: Come, Holy Spirit, guide me.

Leader: When I am afraid to do what is right,

All: Come, Holy Spirit, guide me.

Leader: When I need to help others,

All: Come, Holy Spirit, guide me.

 Sing "The Holy Spirit"

The Holy Spirit, sent from God above.
The Holy Spirit, bringing peace and love.
Receive the power of the Holy Spirit today!

The Holy Spirit, giving strength each day.
The Holy Spirit, showing us the way.
Receive the power of the Holy Spirit
today!

© 2008, John Burland. All rights reserved.

Chapter 11 Review

A **Work with Words** Circle the correct answer to complete each sentence.

1. Jesus promised to send ____.

    the Church   the Holy Spirit

2. The Holy Spirit guides the ____.

    Church   animals

3. The Holy Spirit is the ____ Divine Person of the Trinity.

    First   Third

4. The Holy Spirit gives us ____ to guide us.

    Gifts   time

B **Check Understanding** Write the answers to the questions.

5. Who did Jesus send to guide us?

_____

_ _

_____

6. What is one way you can follow the Holy Spirit?

_____

_ _

_____

_ _

_____

Go to **aliveinchrist.osv.com** for an interactive review.

FAMILY+FAITH
LIVING AND LEARNING TOGETHER

YOUR CHILD LEARNED >>>

This chapter explores Jesus' promise to send the Holy Spirit—the Third Divine Person of the Holy Trinity—to guide the Church.

God's Word

 Read **John 14:15–26** to learn how the Holy Spirit is always with us.

Catholics Believe

- God the Holy Spirit is the Third Person of the Holy Trinity.
- The Holy Spirit fills people's hearts with love and guides the Church.

To learn more, go to the *Catechism of the Catholic Church* #737–741 at **usccb.org**.

People of Faith

This week, your child met Saint Rose of Lima. Rose used the Gifts of the Holy Spirit to live a holy life in seventeenth century Peru.

CHILDREN AT THIS AGE >>>

How They Understand the Holy Spirit Even in the most general terms, "God" and "Trinity" are abstract concepts for first-grade children, but the Holy Spirit tends to be the most elusive of all. It's difficult for children this age to grasp this Person of the Trinity who also dwells within the hearts of all Christians. You can help make this more concrete by referring to Gifts and Fruits of the Holy Spirit. It will also help if your child understands that the Holy Spirit helps us to make good choices and prompts us to be loving toward others.

CONSIDER THIS >>>

Do you remember a time when you really needed a guide?

Maybe the journey was long, or the best of directions were still not clear. A good guide can lessen frustration, get you where you need to be, or in some cases give you information you didn't know. The Holy Spirit guides the Church. Whenever you need direction, or you seek to know God's will in your life, remember—"We do not work alone. The Holy Spirit is our teacher and guide" (*USCCA, p.16*).

LET'S TALK >>>

- Ask your child to share a time when he or she was guided or helped.
- Share about a time when the Holy Spirit guided you or helped you pray.

LET'S PRAY >>>

 Saint Rose, pray for us that we may always use the Gifts of the Holy Spirit in our lives. Amen.

 For a multimedia glossary of Catholic Faith Words, Sunday readings, seasonal and Saint resources, and chapter activities go to **aliveinchrist.osv.com**.

Friends of God

 Let Us Pray

Leader: We trust in you always, O Lord.

"Blessed the man who sets
his security in the LORD." Psalm 40:5

All: We trust in you always, O Lord. Amen.

 **God's Word**

"But I say to you, love your enemies, and pray for those who persecute you, that you may be children of your heavenly Father."

Matthew 5:44–45

? What Do You Wonder?

- Who do you trust?
- When has it been hard to show kindness?

Getting Started

Catholic Faith Words

Here are the vocabulary words for this chapter:

- Saint
- angel
- holy

In this chapter you will learn that Saints are heroes of the Church who loved God very much, led holy lives, and are with God in Heaven. You will also learn that Saints show us how to live holy lives.

Use the chart below to name some people you know who serve God with love.

 Write about or draw three people you know who lead holy lives.

Holy People I Know

Activity

God's Friends The Saints are friends of God who've led holy lives. Look at the pictures below and circle the ways you can show you are God's friend, too.

Keep all the toys for yourself.

Treat everyone with kindness.

Help when someone needs you.

Ignore your parents.

Jesus visits the home of two sisters named Martha and Mary.

Underline what Saints did more than anything.

Holy People

What does Jesus ask you to do?

Saints are God's friends and heroes of the Church. They led holy lives here on Earth. They showed their love for God more than anything. They now live forever with God and the **angels** in Heaven.

You can learn from the Bible how to be God's friend.

 God's Word

Martha and Mary

Jesus visited two sisters named Martha and Mary. Mary sat next to Jesus and listened to everything he said. Martha did all the cooking and cleaning. She was doing all the work! Martha started to get angry with her sister.

© Our Sunday Visitor

Martha said to Jesus, "Mary is making me do all the work. Please tell her to help me!" Jesus told Martha not to worry. He said that Mary was doing the most important thing which was to listen to him. **Based on Luke 10:38–42**

Family of Saints

Saints are **holy** people. They are set apart for God and are filled with the Holy Spirit. Holy people serve God with love.

Catholics celebrate many Saints. You are part of the Catholic Church and her family of Saints! You are connected to the Saints who lived before you. You are also connected to holy people who live now.

Catholic Faith Words

Saint a hero of the Church who loved God very much, led a holy life, and is now with God in Heaven.

angel a type of spiritual being that does God's work, such as delivering messages from God or helping to keep people safe from harm

holy unique and pure; set apart for God and his purposes

Saint Anthony

Think Write the name of someone you know who serves God.

Mary

Share Tell a classmate about this person. Talk about ways you can serve God.

All Kinds of Saints

How do Saints show their love?

Stories about the Saints help you learn how to be holy. Saints are heroes of the Church. They loved God very much and led holy lives. Mary, the Mother of Jesus, is the first and greatest of the Saints.

Mary is the Mother of God, and our Mother, too. She loves and cares for us just as she did for Jesus.

➡ **How can we thank Mary for her love?**

A Simple Man

Saint Juan Diego was visited by Our Lady of Guadalupe on his way to Mass. He spent the rest of his life sharing his story with others.

A King

Saint Louis IX of France was a powerful man. He used his position as king to help care for the sick and less fortunate. He served meals near his palace to people in need.

The Daughter of a Warrior

Saint Kateri Tekakwitha is the first Native American to become a Saint. She devoted her life to prayer, penance, and those who were sick or old.

Activity

Matching Read the descriptions below. Match each description with a holy person on these pages. Write the number in the box next to the person's picture.

1. Used his position to help feed and take care of others.

2. Shared his vision with others.

3. Devoted herself to a life of prayer and penance.

Our Catholic Life

How can you be a Saint?

Saints are not just people who lived along time ago. God wants you to be a Saint, too! You are God's friend. Jesus shows you how to be holy, and the Holy Spirit helps you live a holy life every day.

Our Catholic Tradition
For more, go to page **382**

Here are some ways you can show that you are God's friend.

Place an X next to the things you do already.

Ways to Be God's Friend

 Think about other people, not just yourself.

 Treat everyone with kindness.

 Help when someone needs you.

 Pray every day.

 Learn more about God.

 Try your best to do what is right.

 Love others as Jesus did.

People of Faith

Saint Dominic, 1170–1221

Saint Dominic was a very good speaker. He told people about Jesus. When he talked about God, people came from all over to listen. They wanted to be holy like Dominic. He said that hearing about God wasn't enough. He said that if you want to be holy, you need to praise God and bless other people. He also said that it is more important to be good and do the right thing than to talk all the time.

August 8

Discuss: What good thing have you done today?

Learn more about Saint Dominic at **aliveinchrist.osv.com**

Activity

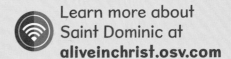

Being a Saint Color the X's red and the O's another color to find the hidden message.

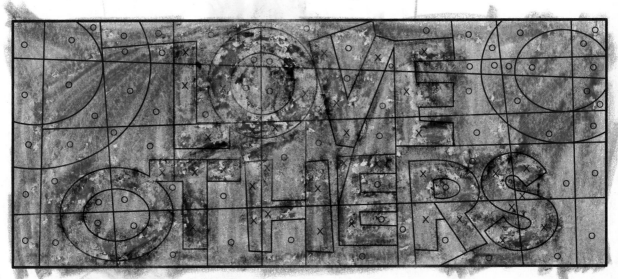

Litany of the Saints

Gather and begin with the Sign of the Cross.

Leader: When we pray with the Saints, we ask them to pray with us and for us. Holy Mary,

All: pray for us.

Leader: Saint Juan Diego,

All: pray for us.

Leader: Saint Louis IX,

All: pray for us.

Leader: Saint Kateri,

All: pray for us.

▶ Sing "Oh, When the Saints"

Oh, when the saints go marching in;
Oh, when the saints go marching in;
Oh, Lord, I want to be
in that number,
when the saints go
marching in.

© Our Sunday Visitor

Chapter 12 Review

A **Work with Words** Circle the correct answer.

1. The greatest Saint is _Mary_.

   Saint Louis IX   (Mary)

2. To be holy means to be set apart for _God_.

   (God)   Mary

3. You are _____.

   God's Father   (God's friend)

B **Check Understanding** Write the answers to the questions.

4. What do we call heroes of the Church who loved God, lived holy lives, and are now with God in Heaven?

   Saints

5. What do we call the spiritual beings that do God's work?

   Angels

Go to **aliveinchrist.osv.com** for an interactive review.

FAMILY+FAITH
LIVING AND LEARNING TOGETHER

YOUR CHILD LEARNED >>>

This chapter explains how Saints are people who loved God very much, did his work on Earth, and are with him in Heaven.

God's Word

 Read **Matthew 5:44–45** to learn how God wants us to love those who mistreat us.

Catholics Believe

- Saints are heroes of the Church who can show us how to live.
- People in the Church are called to live holy lives, as Mary and all the Saints did.

To learn more, go to the *Catechism of the Catholic Church* #956–958 at **usccb.org**.

People of Faith

This week, your child met Saint Dominic, the founder of the Order of Preachers, called the Dominicans, whose special gifts help them spread the Gospel.

CHILDREN AT THIS AGE >>>

How They Understand Holy People Every child has heroes. Some "heroes" are better examples than others. "Heroes" can also differ in their longevity. The Saints, on the other hand, are great examples, and they have staying power. Children can relate to Saints because they are real people who lived the Catholic life in their own time and situation. In order to fully take advantage of the great examples Saints can be, it's important that kids have an opportunity to learn not only of their extraordinary virtue, but also the ways in which the Saints' daily lives were ordinary. This helps us to relate and connect with the Saints as real human beings.

CONSIDER THIS >>>

How does your child feel when he or she is chosen to do something special?

When a teacher or coach gives your child an opportunity to let his/her gifts or talents shine, it is a real moment of joy. How different our lives would be if we were more conscious that God has called each of us to use the gifts and talents he has given us to transform the world. "God calls all the members of the Church to fidelity to the union with him begun at Baptism and continued in the other Sacraments" (*USCCA, p. 146*). We are indeed chosen and it should give us joy.

LET'S TALK >>>

- Talk about your favorite Saints. Who were they and what did they do?
- Ask your child to think of some ways he or she can live a holy life.

LET'S PRAY >>>

 Saint Dominic, pray for us that we may be good listeners when people tell us about God. Amen.

 For a multimedia glossary of Catholic Faith Words, Sunday readings, seasonal and Saint resources, and chapter activities go to **aliveinchrist.osv.com**.

A **Work with Words** Fill in the blank to complete the sentence.

1. The ___kingdom___ of God is the world of love, peace, and justice that is in Heaven and is still being built on Earth.

2. The ___holy spirit___ guides the Church.

3. ___saints___ are people who loved God very much, led holy lives, and are now with God in Heaven.

Draw a line from Column A to the best ending in Column B.

Column A	Column B
4. The sign of God's promise to Noah was	treating everyone with kindness.
5. The Church shares Jesus' message about	a rainbow.
6. You can show you are God's friend by	God's Kingdom.

B **Check Understanding** Write the answers to the questions.

7. What did Jesus promise his followers?

He would send the Holy spirit.

8. How did Noah say "yes" to God?

He built an ark It

9. How does the Holy Spirit help you?

gied you

10. Why are Saints called holy?

becaues they listend to God

C **Make Connections** Draw one way to show a welcoming heart.

11.

Morality

Our Catholic Tradition

- Jesus' words and actions teach us that we are to love and serve God and others. (CCC, 1721)

- The Ten Commandments are laws from God that tell us how to love God and others. (CCC, 2067)

- Sometimes we sin, but God always offers forgiveness when we are truly sorry. (CCC, 605, 982)

- God wants us to forgive others and forgive ourselves. (CCC, 1968)

Our Catholic Life

- Disciples follow Jesus when they live and love by his example. (CCC, 1823)

- The Ten Commandments help us know how to show love for God and for others. (CCC, 2069)

- When we sin or make bad choices, we hurt others and ourselves. We need to show we are sorry, ask for forgiveness, and pray for help to do better. (CCC, 734, 1435)

Why does God give us Commandments?

Disciples Serve

 Let Us Pray

Leader: O Lord, teach me how to help others.

"I sing of mercy and justice;
   to you, LORD, I sing praise."   Psalm 101:1

All: O Lord, teach me how to help others.
Amen.

📖 God's Word

The greatest among you must be your servant. Whoever thinks they are more important than someone else is wrong. Whoever thinks everyone is important is right.   Based on Matthew 23:11–12

❓ What Do You Wonder?

- How do you serve your friends?

- What do you do to serve your family?

Getting Started

Catholic Faith Words

Here are the vocabulary words for this chapter:

- serve
- disciple

In this chapter you will learn that Jesus used words and actions to teach us how to serve God. You will also learn that helping and serving others are ways to serve God.

Use the space below to show what you already know about helping other people.

Write or draw words and actions followers of Jesus use to help other people.

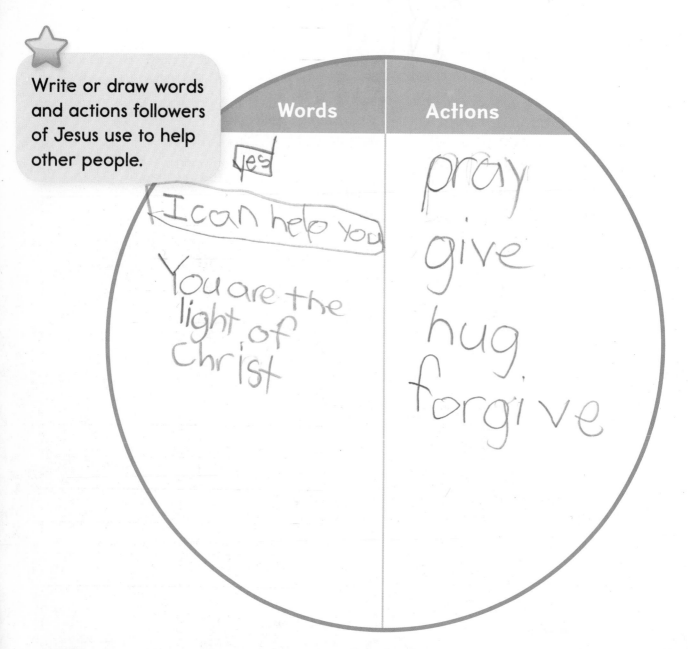

Words	Actions
yes	pray
I can help you	give
You are the light of Christ	hug
	forgive

Love and Serve In the spaces below, name how the people in each picture are serving or being served.

1.

talking to prist

2.

Giveing

3.

reading

Jesus the Servant

What does it mean to serve others?

Jesus taught people to **serve** by helping others in a loving way. We learn from this Bible story that sometimes this surprised them.

Catholic Faith Words

serve to help or give others what they need in a loving way

Underline what Jesus did to teach his followers.

 God's Word

The Washing of the Disciples' Feet

One night Jesus shared a special meal with his followers. During supper, Jesus got up and tied a towel around his waist. He poured water into a basin. Jesus washed and dried his disciples' feet. His followers were surprised to see their teacher do the work of a servant.

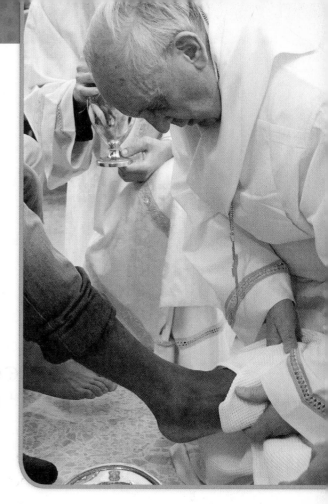

Jesus told them that if he would wash their feet that they should do the same and wash another's feet. He told them to serve others.

Based on John 13:2–17

Serve Like Jesus

Jesus served his followers. He taught them to serve others. Good helpers serve with love in their hearts. You can serve others in many ways.

Activity

Think Draw a picture of something you can do to help, or serve, people in your neighborhood.

Share your idea with a classmate.

© Our Sunday Visitor

Disciples of Jesus

How can you be a follower of Jesus?

Catholic Faith Words

disciple a follower of Jesus who believes in him and lives by his teachings

Jesus used more than words to teach about God's love and how to serve others. He used actions, too. He showed people how to trust in his Father and help others.

You are a **disciple** of Jesus. This means you believe in him and follow his example. Jesus helped others.

➜ How can you be a helper to those around you?

Draw one way someone else has helped you.

© Our Sunday Visitor

Serve God and Others

Serving others made Jesus happy. Jesus served others with a kind heart. You can serve by letting others choose first or go ahead of you in line. You can serve by listening when someone needs a friend. When you serve, you can show God's love.

God the Father asks you to serve with a kind, happy heart. By serving others, you serve him. He wants you to be the best you can be. By developing good habits, your actions can make others happy.

Our Catholic Tradition

For more, go to page **375**

© Our Sunday Visitor

Activity

Word Search Use the Word List to find the words in the Word Search. Circle each word when you find it.

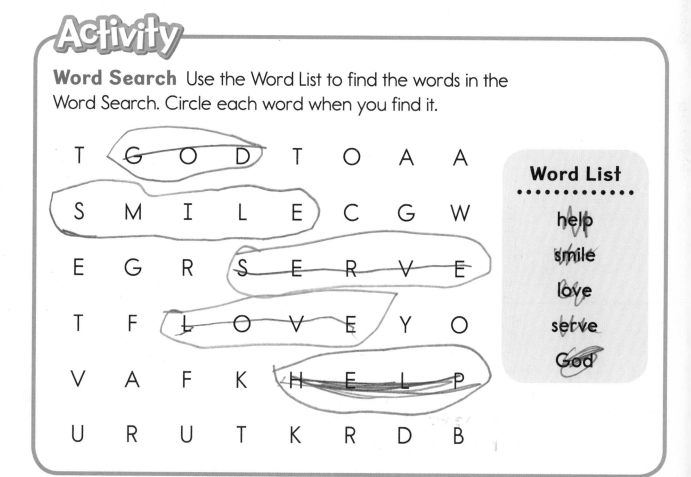

T	G	O	D	T	O	A	A
S	M	I	L	E	C	G	W
E	G	R	S	E	R	V	E
T	F	L	O	V	E	Y	O
V	A	F	K	H	E	L	P
U	R	U	T	K	R	D	B

Word List

help
smile
love
serve
God

Our Catholic Life

How can you follow Jesus and serve others?

Jesus gave his friends an example of how to serve others. He said, "Follow me. Do what I do."

Following Jesus doesn't just mean washing people's feet. There are many ways to follow Jesus and serve others with love. Here are some ideas.

Place a check mark next to the things you would like to do.

Follow Jesus and Serve Others

 Hug someone who is lonely.

 Share food with someone who is hungry.

 Give a coat to someone who is cold.

 Cheer up someone who is sad.

 Help someone up who has fallen down.

People of Faith

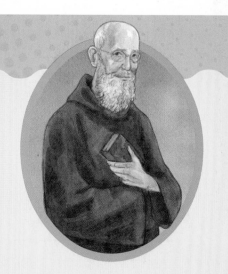

**Venerable Father Solanus Casey,
1870–1957**

Solanus Casey wanted to be a priest, but
he couldn't be a regular priest because he
didn't get good grades in school. He asked
God to show him how he could best serve
others. Father Solanus listened to people
and helped them with their problems.
Many people were cured of sickness
when Father Solanus prayed for them.

Discuss: What can you do to help
one of your friends today?

Learn more about
Father Solanus Casey
at **aliveinchrist.osv.com**

Activity

Match the Actions Match one way that you
could help the people in the pictures.

**Be kind to someone
who is lonely**

Help pick up

A Promise Prayer

Gather and begin with the Sign of the Cross.

Leader: Jesus said, "I am among you as the one who serves." Luke 22:27

Follow in Jesus' footsteps. Pray to be one who serves.

Leader: When someone needs a friend,

All: I will follow Jesus and serve.

Leader: When a job at home needs doing,

All: I will follow Jesus and serve.

Leader: When someone needs cheering up,

All: I will follow Jesus and serve.

Leader: When anyone needs help,

All: I will follow Jesus and serve.

▶ **All:** Sing "Jesus in the Morning"
Jesus, Jesus,
Jesus in the morning,
Jesus at the noontime;
Jesus, Jesus, Jesus when
the sun goes down!

Chapter 13 Review

A **Work with Words** Draw a heart next to each sentence that tells about a person who is serving.

1. ☒ Elena sees her teacher carrying a big stack of books. Elena walks away.

2. ♡ A child is hurt on the playground. Trevor leads the crying child to a teacher.

3. ♡ Alison sets the table for supper.

B **Check Understanding** Circle the best answer.

4. Jesus washed his friends' feet as a sign of ___.

   (serving)   playing

5. When you serve others, you show your ___ for God.

   hope   (love)

6. God the Father wants you to be a ___ of Jesus.

   leader   (disciple)

7. Name one way to serve God and others.

   Help other.

Go to **aliveinchrist.osv.com** for an interactive review.

FAMILY+FAITH
LIVING AND LEARNING TOGETHER

YOUR CHILD LEARNED >>>

This chapter identifies a disciple as a follower of Jesus who believes in him, lives by his teaching, and connects serving others with serving God.

God's Word

 Read **Matthew 23:11–12** to learn who is truly greatest in God's eyes, the one seated at the table or the one who serves.

Catholics Believe

• Jesus' words and actions teach us how to love and serve God.

• When you serve others, you are serving God.

To learn more, go to the *Catechism of the Catholic Church* #1822–1827 at **usccb.org**.

People of Faith

This week, your child met Venerable Father Solanus Casey. He spent his life serving others in the humble job of doorkeeper.

CHILDREN AT THIS AGE >>>

How They Understand Serving Others Because they are naturally more focused on their own needs than on the needs of others, first-graders might sometimes fail to notice the ways in which they might be of help to another person. You can help your child with this by pointing out times when someone needs help or support and encouraging your child to think of some ways to be of service. It might also help to offer a few suggestions if he or she is unable to come up with ideas on his or her own.

CONSIDER THIS >>>

What motivates you to help others?

We all have different reasons for acting with charity. As Christians, however, we are united by the understanding that we are of service to one another because we have been united to Christ in Baptism and we act in his name. "In this communion of the Church, the members are called to love God, others, and self, and so to be a communal witness of the love by which Christ saved the world. By divine love, we are joined to the communion of the Father, Son, and Holy Spirit" (*USCCA, p. 119*).

LET'S TALK >>>

• Talk about how Jesus washed his friends' feet and how they might have felt to have received his kindness.

• Ask your child to think of someone in your neighborhood who could use help. What kinds of things can you and your family do to help this person?

LET'S PRAY >>>

 Dear God, help us do our chores without complaining. Amen.

 For a multimedia glossary of Catholic Faith Words, Sunday readings, seasonal and Saint resources, and chapter activities go to **aliveinchrist.osv.com**.

Making Choices

 Let Us Pray

Leader: God, please help us make good choices.

"Be kind to your servant that I may live,
that I may keep your word."
Psalm 119:17

All: God, help us make good choices. Amen.

 God's Word

A man asked Jesus, "Teacher, what must I do to receive eternal life?"

Jesus replied, "What is written in the law?"

The man answered, "Love the Lord your God with all your heart, with all your being, with all your strength, and with all your mind and your neighbor as yourself."

"You have answered correctly," Jesus said. "Do this and you will live."
Based on Luke 10:25–28

? What Do You Wonder?

- Why is Jesus called "Teacher"?
- Why is it sometimes hard to make good choices?

Getting Started

In this chapter you will learn that the Ten Commandments are God's laws that tell us how to love him and others. You will also learn that God gives us free will to choose how we will behave.

Use the chart below to show what you know about making choices.

Catholic Faith Words

Here are the vocabulary words for this chapter:

- Ten Commandments
- obey
- free will

 Draw a line to match the choices that lead you to God and the choices that lead you away from God.

Where Our Choices Lead	
Choice	**Leads You**
Praying and Going to Mass	• To God
Saying Mean Things	• Away From God
Following the Rules	• To God
Disobeying Your Parents	• Away From God
Telling a Lie	• To God
Listening to Your Teacher	• Away From God

What's Next? Read about each situation and answer the questions.

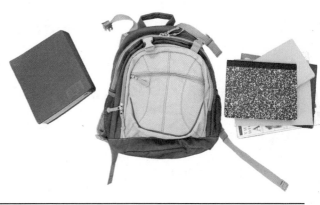

1. Hannah sees a friend drop her book bag and everything falls out. What choices does Hannah have?

_____

- -

_____

- -

_____

- -

_____

2. Hector is standing in line. The boy behind him trips and falls into him. What choices does Hector have?

_____

- -

_____

- -

_____

- -

_____

Types of Choices

How does God help us make choices?

Some choices are easy to make. If you are choosing between two kinds of healthful foods, both choices are good ones. Making this kind of choice will not hurt you or anyone else.

Other choices are hard to make. Sometimes it can be difficult to choose between right and wrong. The choices you make can help others or hurt them.

Circle how your choices can affect others.

➡ **What are some choices children your age make?**

A Gift from God

Long ago, God wanted to help his People know how to live. He gave the **Ten Commandments** to a special man named Moses. Moses helped the people understand God's laws. These laws still help us make good choices. The Ten Commandments are listed on page 314 of your book.

Catholic Faith Words

Ten Commandments
God's laws that tell people how to love him and others

 God's Word

God's Commandments

Moses said, "What does the Lord, your God, ask of you? God wants you to respect him and to follow him. The Lord your God wants you to love and serve him with all your heart and all your soul. God wants you to obey his commandments and teachings."
Based on Deuteronomy 10:12–13

Our Catholic Tradition
For more, go to page 374

Activity

Think What are some of God's teachings?

Share As a class, talk about what God asks us to do.

© Our Sunday Visitor

Good Choices

How do your choices affect you and others?

© Our Sunday Visitor

God created you to be free. You can choose to **obey** God. When you do what God asks, you choose what is good and you grow closer to God. Bad choices make you turn away from God.

Being able to choose whether to obey God or disobey God is called **free will**. God created us with free will because he wants us to choose good.

The Ten Commandments can help you use your free will to make loving choices.

Catholic Faith Words

obey to do things or act in certain ways that are requested by those in authority

free will being able to choose whether to obey God or disobey God. God created us with free will because he wants us to make good choices.

Steps to Good Choices

1. Think about whether your choice shows love for God and others.

2. Ask yourself and others if your choice follows the Ten Commandments and things Jesus would do.

3. Pray to the Holy Spirit to guide you.

Consequences

All choices have consequences, or results. Bad choices have consequences that can hurt you or others. Good choices have good consequences. They help you show love and respect for yourself, others, and God.

Good choices have good results for you and others.

Activity

Good or Bad? Circle the picture that shows the good choice.

Our Catholic Life

How can you keep the Ten Commandments?

The Ten Commandments help you know how to show love for God and for others. Here are some ways you can keep the Commandments.

Living The Ten Commandments

1. Love God more than anyone or anything.

2. Use God's name with respect.

3. Take time to pray. Go to Mass with your family on Sundays, or Saturday evenings.

4. Love your family. Treat everyone in your family kindly. Obey the rules.

5. Stay away from fighting. Find peaceful ways to solve problems.

6. Respect your body and the bodies of others. Think about the way you speak and act.

7. Care for other people's things. Take care of what you have.

8. Be honest. Say only good things about people.

9. Be true to family members and friends.

10. Be thankful for what you have.

1. Circle the Commandments that focus on loving God.

2. Underline the ones that focus on loving others and yourself.

People of Faith

Saint Frances Cabrini, 1850–1917

Saint Frances Cabrini lived in Italy. She wanted to go to China to teach the people there about God. Pope Leo XIII asked her to go the United States instead. Mother Frances had a choice. She decided to obey the Pope. She left Italy and went to the United States where she built schools, orphanages, and hospitals.

November 13

Discuss: Talk about a hard choice you had to make.

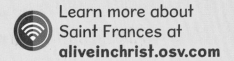

Learn more about Saint Frances at **aliveinchrist.osv.com**

Activity

Choose Read the Ten Commandments on page 374. Pick one Commandment and draw a picture of one way you can follow it this week.

 **Let Us Pray**

A Helping Prayer

Gather and begin with the Sign of the Cross.

Leader: Ask the Holy Spirit for help to make wise and loving choices.

Reader 1: When I forget to put God first,

All: Holy Spirit, help me choose to love.

Reader 2: When I am lazy and do not want to pray,

All: Holy Spirit, help me choose to love.

Reader 3: When I don't feel like listening to my parents,

All: Holy Spirit, help me choose to love.

Reader 4: When I am angry and want to say or do something hurtful,

All: Holy Spirit, help me choose to love.

Reader 5: When I want to take something that doesn't belong to me,

All: Holy Spirit, help me choose to love.

Reader 6: When I think about telling a lie,

All: Holy Spirit, help me choose to love.

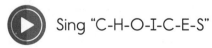 Sing "C-H-O-I-C-E-S"

Chapter 14 Review

A **Work with Words** Circle the correct word to complete each sentence.

1. The Ten Commandments are God's ____.

    laws   stories

2. God gave ____ the Ten Commandments.

    Jesus   Moses

3. I show love for God when I choose what is ____.

    easy   good

4. A bad choice can ____ us and others.

    hurt   help

5. ____ choices have consequences.

    Some   All

6. We ____ God when we do what he asks.

    obey   disobey

B **Check Understanding** Write your answer on the space below.

7. What is being able to choose whether to obey or disobey God called?

_____

- -

_____

Go to aliveinchrist.osv.com for an interactive review.

© Our Sunday Visitor

FAMILY+FAITH
LIVING AND LEARNING TOGETHER

YOUR CHILD LEARNED >>>

This chapter explains free will as a gift from God and the Ten Commandments as God's laws that tell us how to love God and others.

God's Word

 Read **Luke 10:25–28** to find out what Jesus said is the most important Commandment.

Catholics Believe

- The Ten Commandments are God's laws to help people love him and others.
- God gives people the freedom to choose.

To learn more, go to the *Catechism of the Catholic Church* #2056–2060 at **usccb.org**.

People of Faith

This week, your child met Saint Frances Cabrini, the first American citizen to be canonized. Saint Frances wanted to be a missionary to China, but came to the U.S. instead.

CHILDREN AT THIS AGE >>>

How They Understand Making Choices Rules are very important to children in first grade. They are just beginning to understand cause and effect, the idea that the world works according to certain rules, so they tend to form their ideas about various places and situations based on what the rules

are. They also become distressed when someone else is not following the rules, even when it does not directly impact them. You can help your child make good choices by providing him or her with clear, developmentally appropriate, and consistent guidelines for behavior.

CONSIDER THIS >>>

What moves you to do the right thing, to choose what is good?

Sometimes we know the right thing to do, but we aren't brave enough or motivated enough to do so. Living in right relationship with God helps us to live in right relationship with others. The Holy Spirit will give you the grace to do God's will. "The moral life requires grace...the grace that comes to us from Christ in the Spirit is as essential as love and rules and, in fact, makes love and keeping the rules possible" (*USCCA, p. 318*).

LET'S TALK >>>

- Ask your child to talk about some choices he or she has made recently.
- Talk about doing something you didn't want to do at first, but that later turned out to be the right thing to do.

LET'S PRAY >>>

 Saint Frances Cabrini, pray for us that we may make the right choices and always obey our mothers and fathers. Amen.

For a multimedia glossary of Catholic Faith Words, Sunday readings, seasonal and Saint resources, and chapter activities go to **aliveinchrist.osv.com**.

Showing Sorrow

 Let Us Pray

Leader: May we learn that God forgives us always and forever. Amen.

Create a clean heart for me, O God; renew in me a strong spirit.

Based on Psalm 51:12

All: Thank you, God, for teaching us how to forgive.

God's Word

Peter went up to Jesus and asked, "How many times should I forgive someone who does something wrong to me? Is seven times enough?" Jesus answered: "Not just seven times, but seventy-seven times!" Based on Matthew 18:21–22

? What Do You Wonder?

- Who do you forgive?
- When do you say "I'm sorry"?

Getting Started

Catholic Faith Words

Here is the vocabulary word for this chapter:

- sin

In this chapter you will learn that sin is a choice to disobey God. You will also learn that God forgives people who are sorry. He wants us to forgive others and ourselves.

Use this table to show what you already know about showing you are sorry.

Check off the ways you can show you are sorry.

Ways to Show You Are Sorry

- ✓ Give a hug
- ✗ Blame someone else
- ✗ Ignore the person you hurt
- ✓ Try to do better
- ✓ Say you are sorry
- ✓ Ask for forgiveness
- ✓ Promise to not do it again
- ✗ Yell at the person you hurt

Activity

Making Things Better Unscramble the following words that tell us some things we can do to make things better.

1. **rofevig**

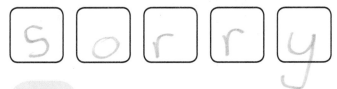
f o r g i v e

2. **ysror**

s o r r y

3. **hgu**

h u g

4. **leims**

s m i l e

5. **lpeh**

h e l p

It is important to take time to think about our choices.

Underline what helps your friendship with God grow stronger.

Obeying God

How can you help your friendship with God stay strong?

When you choose to do something you know is wrong, you disobey God. When you disobey God, you commit a **sin**. Accidents or mistakes are not sins. We do not do them on purpose.

When you sin, it hurts your friendship with God. You also hurt yourself and others when you do not choose to do good.

God wants you to obey him. He asks you to love him and others with your whole heart. When you do this, your friendship with God grows stronger.

© Our Sunday Visitor

Being Sorry

Jesus told a story about how God wants you to act when you are sorry.

 God's Word

The Prodigal Son

Once a father had two sons. The younger son wanted half of his father's money so he could leave home. The father sadly gave the younger son the money.

The son left and wasted all his money. He got a job feeding pigs. He was sad and cold and all alone. The son started to walk home. He hoped that his father would give him a better job.

When the son returned, he cried, "I am sorry I have sinned. I am not good enough to be your son." The father hugged his son and threw a big party.

The older son was angry that his father forgave him. But the father said, "He has come home. We must welcome him."

Based on Luke 15:11–32

© Our Sunday Visitor

Catholic Faith Words

sin a person's choice to disobey God on purpose and do what he or she knows is wrong. Accidents and mistakes are not sins.

Activity

Think about some times when people are selfish.

Share one example with your classmate.

Ask for Forgiveness

How does God know if you are sorry for not obeying him?

Jesus taught that his Father forgives sinners. God forgives us when we are truly sorry and ask his forgiveness through the Church.

God wants you to forgive, too. God wants all people to be friends.

When people forgive, they show love for God and others. When you ask someone to forgive you, you hope the person will say "Yes!"

It's not always easy to forgive someone who has hurt you or made you mad. God wants you to give that person another chance to make things better.

Underline what God wants you to do.

Make Things Better

God wants you to be close to him. When you sin, you can say "I'm sorry. Please forgive me. I will try to make better choices."

God will always say "I forgive you!" God is always ready to forgive you. God's love for you never ends.

➔ **When have you felt God's love?**

Our Catholic Tradition
For more, go to page 365

Activity

Draw an Ending Work with a classmate. Imagine that you have hurt someone's feelings. Draw a way to make things better.

Our Catholic Life

How can you make up for doing something wrong?

When you make a bad choice, you hurt others and yourself. It might seem hard to make things better. The Holy Spirit will help you. Here are some steps to follow.

Making Things Better

1 Think about what you have done. Tell God you are sorry.

2 Tell the person you hurt that you are sorry and ask for forgiveness.

3 Do whatever you can to make up for what you did wrong.

4 Ask the Holy Spirit to help you do better in the future.

People of Faith

Saint Dismas, first century

Saint Dismas was crucified at the same time as Jesus. He knew that he had done bad things. He asked forgiveness for all the things he stole. Then he asked Jesus to remember him in Heaven. Jesus told Saint Dismas that he would be with God in Paradise. Saint Dismas discovered that when we are sorry for our sins, God will always forgive us.

March 25

Discuss: What is the best way to let someone know you are sorry?

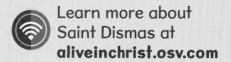

Learn more about Saint Dismas at **aliveinchrist.osv.com**

Activity

Thumbs Up or Down Circle the thumbs up if the words or actions show forgiveness. Circle the thumbs down if they do not.

 Saying you are sorry.

 Saying "no" when someone asks you for forgiveness.

 Asking the person you've hurt for forgiveness.

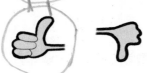 Asking the Holy Spirit to help you do better in the future.

Prayer for Forgiveness

Gather and begin with the Sign of the Cross.

Leader: Together, let us tell God we are sorry and we will try to do better. Repeat after me: My God, I am sorry for my sins with all my heart.

All: (Echo)

Leader: In choosing to do wrong and failing to do good,

All: (Echo)

Leader: I have sinned against you.

All: (Echo)

Leader: I do not want to sin because I love you.

All: (Echo)

Leader: I promise that with your help

All: (Echo)

Leader: I will try to do better. Amen.

All: (Echo)

▶ Sing "Children of God"

A **Work with Words** Write the letter of the word from the Word Bank that completes each sentence.

Word Bank

a. love

b. sin

c. friendship

d. sorry

e. forgive

1. Disobeying God's law is called .

2. When you God, you show your love.

3. You can start over with God by saying I'm .

4. When you sin, you hurt your with God.

5. God will always you.

B **Check Understanding** Number the steps to make things better.

6. ☐ 4   Ask the Holy Spirit to help you do better in the future.

☐ 1   Think about what you have done.

☐ 2   Ask the person you hurt to forgive you.

☐ 3   Do something to make up for it.

 Go to **aliveinchrist.osv.com** for an interactive review.

© Our Sunday Visitor

FAMILY+FAITH
LIVING AND LEARNING TOGETHER

YOUR CHILD LEARNED >>>

This chapter explains the consequences of sin and our need for God's forgiveness.

God's Word

 Read **Matthew 18:21–22** to find out how many times Jesus tells us we need to forgive someone.

Catholics Believe

- God always forgives those who are truly sorry and ask his forgiveness.
- God asks that we forgive others and ourselves.

To learn more, go to the *Catechism of the Catholic Church* #1846–1850 at **usccb.org**.

People of Faith

This week, your child met Saint Dismas, the name given to the good thief who was crucified with Jesus.

CHILDREN AT THIS AGE >>>

How They Understand Saying "I'm Sorry" Many young children are forced to apologize when they have done something wrong even though they may not fully realize the impact their behavior had on the other person. You can help your child make amends sincerely by helping him or her understand what the behavior felt like for the other person. Sometimes it helps to hear from the other person how they felt. Also, a concrete action to help make up for the wrong is often better than words alone.

CONSIDER THIS >>>

Do you find it hard to admit that you've done something wrong?

For many people admitting they are wrong is a serious challenge. They may feel diminished or they may confuse what they did with who they are. As adults, however, we recognize that it is necessary to be honest about our failings or we will never be able to grow. "Confession liberates us from sins that trouble our hearts and makes it possible to be reconciled to God and others. We are asked to look into our souls and, with an honest and unblinking gaze, identify our sins. This opens our minds and hearts to God, moves us toward communion with the Church, and offers us a new future" (*USCCA, p. 238*).

LET'S TALK >>>

- Talk about times when it's been hard to obey God.
- Ask your child to talk about the steps to follow if they make a wrong choice.

LET'S PRAY >>>

 Dear God, help us to always be sorry when we disobey you. Amen.

 For a multimedia glossary of Catholic Faith Words, Sunday readings, seasonal and Saint resources, and chapter activities go to **aliveinchrist.osv.com**.

5 Unit Review

A **Work with Words** Circle the correct word to complete each sentence.

1. Jesus taught his followers to ____ others.

   serve   have fun with

2. The ____ Commandments tell how to love God and others.

   Five   Ten

3. ____ choices help you show love and respect for God and others.

   Bad   Good

4. When you ____ God, you commit a sin.

   disobey   obey

5. Jesus taught that God ____.

   forgets   forgives

B **Check Understanding** Write your answers on the spaces below.

6. Name one way to serve others.

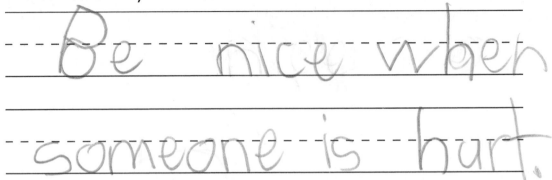

Be nice when someone is hurt.

7. Tell about one Commandment.

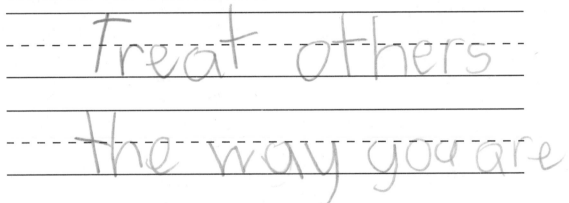

Treat others the way you are

8. Who forgives you when you say, "I'm sorry"?

God and the friend

C **Make Connections** Circle the pictures that show how to follow Jesus.

9.

10. Draw one way you can follow Jesus.

Sacraments

Our Catholic Tradition

- In the Bible, God tells us about his great love for us. (CCC, 231)

- The Seven Sacraments are special signs and celebrations that Jesus gave his Church. The Sacraments allow us to share in the life and work of God. (CCC,1131)

- The Church celebrates the Seven Sacraments as signs of God's love and life. (CCC, 1116)

- Grace means sharing in God's help and life so that we may grow as his children. (CCC, 1996)

How does the grace we receive from the Seven Sacraments help us grow closer to Jesus?

Our Catholic Life

- We can share the Good News of God's love by what we say and how we act. (CCC, 3)

- Each Sacrament is a celebration that uses words and signs that show God's love. (CCC, 1145)

- In Baptism, we are called to be signs of God's life and love. (CCC, 1270)

© Our Sunday Visitor

Jesus the Savior

 Let Us Pray

Leader: Thank you for saving us, Jesus.

"LORD, I call to you; hasten to me;
listen to my plea when I call." Psalm 141:1

All: Thank you for saving us, Jesus. Amen.

 God's Word

"Then the angel said to the women in reply, 'Do not be afraid! I know that you are seeking Jesus the crucified. He is not here, for he has been raised just as he said. Come and see the place where he lay.'" Matthew 28:5–6

? What Do You Wonder?

- Where is Jesus?
- When will you talk with Jesus?

Getting Started

In this chapter you will learn that Adam and Eve chose to disobey God and commit sin. You will also learn that God loved us so much that he sent his Son, Jesus, to be our Savior. Jesus gave his life so that people could have new life with God.

Use this chart to show what you know about how Jesus saved us.

Catholic Faith Words

Here are the vocabulary words for this chapter:

- Original Sin
- Resurrection

 Explain what the pictures represent and why these images are important to us.

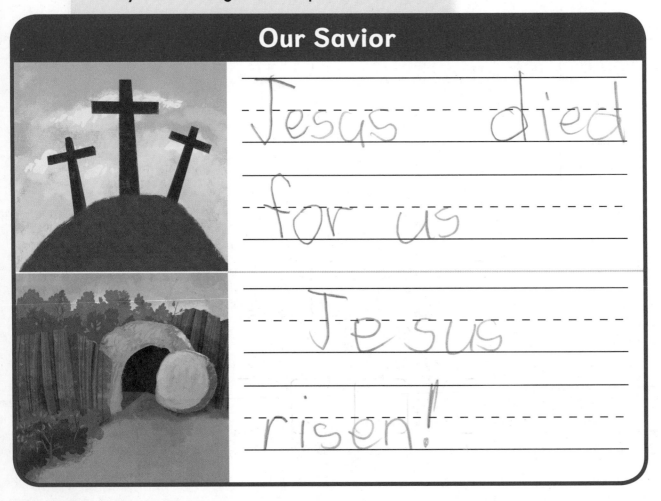

Our Savior

Jesus died for us Jesus risen!

Activity

Solve the Code God the Father sent his Son so that we could know his love. Jesus died for us and rose to new life, we remember this during Lent. Solve the code to find what Jesus' name means.

A=1　　B=2　　C=3　　D=4　　E=5　　F=6

G=7　　H=8　　I=9　　J=10　　K=11　　L=12

M=13　　N=14　　O=15　　P=16　　Q=17　　R=18

S=19　　T=20　　U=21　　V=22　　W=23　　X=24

Y=25　　Z=26

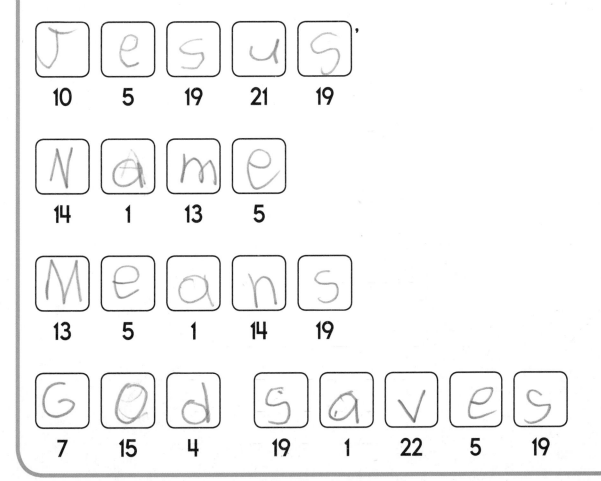

J	e	s	u	s '
10	5	19	21	19

N	a	m	e
14	1	13	5

M	e	a	n	s
13	5	1	14	19

G	o	d	s	a	v	e	s
7	15	4	19	1	22	5	19

Adam and Eve

Why did God's people need to be saved?

God created the first people to be like him. He made them happy and gave them a garden to care for. Then Adam and Eve made a bad choice. They disobeyed God and brought sin into the world. This is called **Original Sin**.

God Loves

Adam and Eve were no longer the kind of people God wanted them to be.

They broke their friendship with him. They suffered, and they missed God.

But God did not stop loving them. He wanted them to love him.

Catholic Faith Words

Original Sin the first sin committed by Adam and Eve and passed down to everyone

Underline what God wanted Adam and Eve to do.

God's Promise

God said, "I love you always. I will show you how much I love you. I will send a Savior to bring you back to me." God kept this promise. He sent his Son, Jesus, to us. Jesus saves all people from sin. He is our Savior.

Think Write the name of the Savior whom God the Father sent to us.

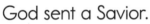

Jesus

Share Talk with a classmate about why God sent a Savior.

New Life with God

How did Jesus save us from sin?

Jesus saved people from the power of sin. He also brought them back to God. Jesus is the Savior.

God's Word

Jesus Lives

Some people did not believe that Jesus was God's Son. He was arrested and nailed to a Cross, where he died. His friends laid his body in a cave and blocked it with a large stone.

Some holy women went to visit the cave where Jesus was laid. The large stone was rolled away. The cave was empty. Two angels said, "Jesus is not here. He is risen from the dead!"

Then Jesus appeared to his followers.

Based on Luke 23–24

> Underline what the two angels said.

© Our Sunday Visitor

Jesus Saves

Jesus' name means, "God saves." He died for all people to save them from their sins. Jesus gave his life so that people could have new life with God.

Jesus being raised from the dead to new life is called the **Resurrection**. He was raised to new life by God the Father through the power of the Holy Spirit.

Jesus being raised to new life is a holy mystery. The Church celebrates the Resurrection in a special way on Easter.

➤ **How do you celebrate Easter?**

Catholic Faith Words

Resurrection the event of Jesus being raised from Death to new life by God the Father through the power of the Holy Spirit

Make Stained Glass Color the letters blue and the surrounding shapes different colors to find who died to save us from our sins.

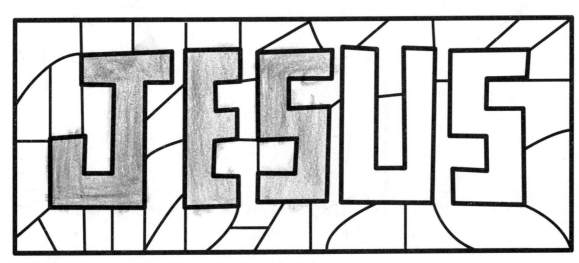

Our Catholic Life

How can you share the Good News of God's love?

After Jesus rose from the dead, he sent his friends to tell everyone the Good News of God's love.

Our Catholic Tradition
For more, go to page **367**

Jesus wants you to share the Good News, too. You can share the Good News by what you say and how you act.

Add a "T" next to the things you will try to do this week.

Ways to Share the Good News

T — Tell someone about Jesus.

T — Invite a friend to come to Mass or a Church event with you.

T — Write a note or draw a picture to cheer up someone who is sad.

T — Treat all people with kindness.

T — Help someone make a good choice.

T — Forgive someone who is sorry for hurting you.

People of Faith

Saint Josephine Bakhita, 1869–1947

Josephine (Giuseppina) Bakhita was born in Africa. At twelve, she was kidnapped and made a slave. She was a slave for many years. When she grew up, she stayed in a convent in Italy. She learned about Jesus there. She discovered that God loves us so much he died for us and wanted to help other people learn about Jesus, too. She became a religious sister and helped prepare missionaries to go to Africa.

February 8

Discuss: How can you let someone know more about Jesus?

 Learn more about Saint Josephine Bakhita at **aliveinchrist.osv.com**

Activity

Tell the Good News Write the words you would use to tell the Good News.

Thank

God

Prayer of Praise

Gather and begin with the Sign of the Cross.

All: Jesus is Savior. Alleluia!

Leader: Save us, Savior of the world,
for by your Cross
and Resurrection,
you have set us free.
Mystery of Faith

All: Jesus is Savior. Alleluia!

Sing and sign a favorite Alleluia.

All: Jesus is Savior. Our hearts are filled
with thanks.

▶ Sing "Savior of the World"

Save us, Lord, for you are
the savior of the world.
© 2011, John Burland.
All rights reserved.

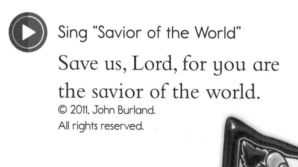

A **Work with Words** Complete each sentence with the letter of the correct word or words from the Word Bank.

Word Bank

a. loves

b. Savior

c. Original Sin

d. happy

e. Resurrection

1. Adam and Eve disobeyed God and committed [c].

2. God always [a] his People.

3. The [e] is the name for Jesus' being raised from Death to new life.

4. Jesus is the [b].

5. God made people to be [d] with him.

B **Check Understanding** Circle the correct answers.

6. Jesus' name means ____.

   God cares   (God saves)

7. Jesus wants you to share ____.

   (the Good News)   sin

8. Jesus saves people from ____.

   work   (the power of sin)

Go to **aliveinchrist.osv.com** for an interactive review.

YOUR CHILD LEARNED >>>

This chapter explains Original Sin and the need for a Savior. It covers Jesus' Death and Resurrection and explains Jesus' sacrifice as a gift of love.

God's Word

 Read **Matthew 28:5–6** to find out what the angel said to those looking for Jesus.

Catholics Believe

- Even though humans sinned, God continued to love us and sent his Son to save us.
- Jesus died and rose to new life, bringing us back to his Father.

To learn more, go to the *Catechism of the Catholic Church* #639–642 at **usccb.org**.

People of Faith

This week, your child met Saint Josephine Bakhita, a former slave from Africa who became a religious sister in Italy.

CHILDREN AT THIS AGE >>>

How They Understand Jesus as Savior Children in first grade will have difficulty understanding the idea that Jesus gave his life as a sacrifice for us. However, they can understand that Jesus loved us so much that he wanted to show us how to live even though it meant he would die. First-graders are just beginning to grasp the permanence of death, making them particularly open to the Gospel message, which says that death could not hold Jesus, and he is risen.

CONSIDER THIS >>>

Have you ever thought about how the way you live your daily life is connected to Jesus' sacrifice?

It can be hard to grasp the importance of what Christ did for us, even for adults. It may seem impossible to live your life in a way that lives up to Jesus' sacrifice. Through our lives, our sufferings, our prayer and work, we are united with Christ. The important sacrifices that we make for each other and for God in our individual lives remind us of the importance of his sacrifice. "In a self-centered culture where people are taught to extend themselves only for something in return, the sacrifices each of us make, following the example of Jesus, who freely sacrificed his life in love for all, point to the reality and power of God's love for us" (*USCCA, p. 221*).

LET'S TALK >>>

- Talk about the ways we celebrate Jesus' Resurrection.
- Ask your child what he or she thinks about Jesus' sacrifice for us.

LET'S PRAY >>>

 Dear God, help us to share your love with everyone we meet, like Saint Josephine did. Amen.

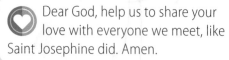 For a multimedia glossary of Catholic Faith Words, Sunday readings, seasonal and Saint resources, and chapter activities go to **aliveinchrist.osv.com**.

Holy Signs

 Let Us Pray

Leader: God, we thank you for the gift of love.

"May the peoples praise you, God;
   may all the peoples praise you!"
Psalm 67:6

All: God, we thank you for the gift of love.
Amen.

 **God's Word**

"You will realize that I am in my Father and you are in me and I in you."   John 14:20

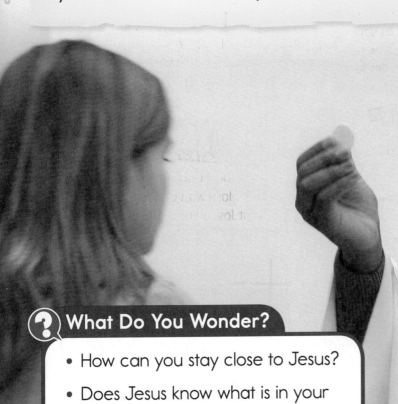

? What Do You Wonder?

- How can you stay close to Jesus?
- Does Jesus know what is in your heart and in your mind?

Getting Started

In this chapter you will learn that the Seven Sacraments are special signs and celebrations that Jesus gave his Church. You will also learn that the Sacraments celebrate that Jesus is still with us, sharing his life and love.

Use this chart to show signs of love that help you find your way.

 Write or draw some signs of love that help you.

Signs of Love That Help Me

Heart means love \ Love	The cross means Jesus died.	The soar aword It mean are meyey Soar aword

Activity

Words and Signs Signs are all around us. What do you think each of these signs represent? Draw a line to the direction that the sign is giving.

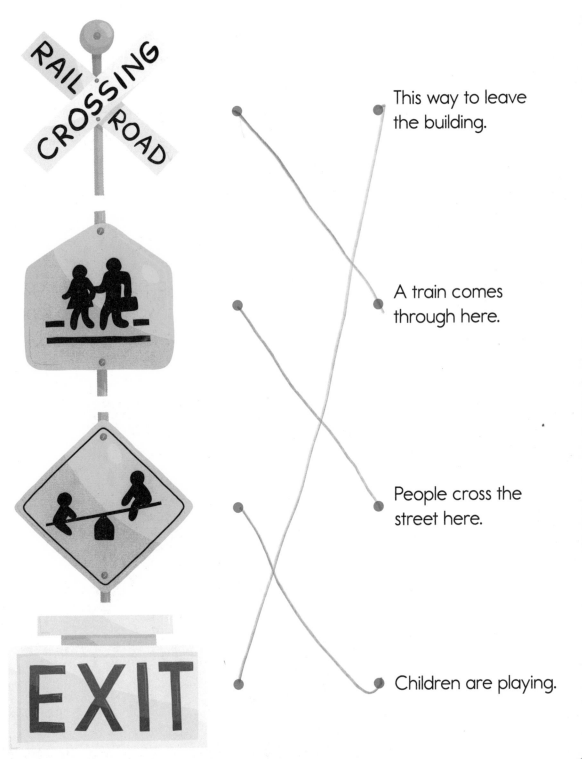

This way to leave the building.

A train comes through here.

People cross the street here.

Children are playing.

Signs of Love

How does the Church show and celebrate God's love?

You read about God's love in the Bible. You learn about God's love from Jesus. Jesus healed people as a sign of his Father's love.

Circle what Jesus said to his followers.

 God's Word

The Advocate

Jesus wanted to remain with his followers even when he returned to God the Father. This is what he said to them:

"I will not leave you orphans; I will come to you. In a little while the world will no longer see me, but you will see me, because I live and you will live." John 14:18–19

Our
Catholic
Tradition
For more,
go to page
364

The Sacraments

God's love is something to celebrate.
Jesus teaches that God is always with you!

The Holy Spirit fills you with God's
love. When you show God's love to other
people, the Holy Spirit is in you.

Jesus gave the Church special signs
to help people celebrate that he is still
here. These signs are called the **Seven
Sacraments**.

Catholic Faith Words

Seven Sacraments
special signs and
celebrations that Jesus
gave his Church. The
Sacraments allow us
to share in the life and
work of God.

Activity

Think What are some pictures or items that
remind you of God?

Share your answer with a classmate.

© Our Sunday Visitor

Signs and Celebrations

How is Jesus with us today?

Jesus gives us Sacraments so that we can always know his love and care.

The Sacraments are special signs and celebrations. Every Sacrament has words and actions we do and things God does that we can't see. When we celebrate the Seven Sacraments, Jesus is with us. The Holy Spirit makes him present to us.

Sacraments of Initiation

- ✓ Baptism
- ✓ Confirmation
- ✓ Eucharist

Sacraments of Healing

- ✓ Penance and Reconciliation
- ✓ Anointing of the Sick

Sacraments at the Service of Communion

- Matrimony
- Holy Orders

Activity

Draw a Sacrament you have taken part in or have seen.

Our Catholic Life

What signs are used to celebrate the Seven Sacraments?

The Church celebrates Seven Sacraments. Each Sacrament uses words and signs that show God's love.

Place a check mark next to the Sacraments and signs you have seen.

Sacraments		Signs	
☐ Baptism	Water	Water	God gives new life in Jesus.
☐ Confirmation		Holy Oil (Chrism)	The gifts of the Holy Spirit are given.
☐ Eucharist		Bread and Wine	The Body and Blood of Christ are present.
☐ Penance and Reconciliation		Outstretched Hand	God forgives those who are sorry.
☐ Anointing of the Sick		Oil of the Sick	God helps heal our bodies and spirits.
☐ Matrimony		Wedding Rings	God blesses the love of a man and woman.
☐ Holy Orders		Holy Oil (Chrism)	God calls men to lead and serve the Church.

© Our Sunday Visitor

People of Faith

Mary, first century

Mary is the Mother of Jesus. She is the greatest of all Saints. One day an angel gave Mary a message: "You will have a son named Jesus." Mary was confused. She asked, "How can this be done?" The angel said, "The Holy Spirit will come upon you. Your son will be the Son of God." The Holy Spirit was with Mary. The Spirit is with us, too, in the Sacraments.

January 1

Discuss: What Sacraments have you received?

Learn more about Mary at **aliveinchrist.osv.com**

Match the Signs Match the Sacraments on the left with the correct symbols on the right.

Baptism •   •

Eucharist •   •

Penance and
Reconciliation •   •

Matrimony •   •

 **Let Us Pray**

Prayer of Thanks

Gather and begin with the Sign of the Cross.

Leader: For Baptism's life-giving water,

All: Thank you, Jesus.

Leader: For holy oil that blesses,

All: Thank you, Jesus.

Leader: For the gift of your life in the Eucharist,

All: Thank you, Jesus.

▶ Sing "The Seven Sacraments"

The Sacraments,
the Seven Sacraments.
Signs that come from Jesus
and give us grace.
The Sacraments,
the Seven Sacraments.
Signs that God is with us
in a special way.
© 2008, John Burland. All rights reserved.

Chapter 17 Review

A **Work with Words** Complete each sentence with the letter of the correct word or words from the Word Bank.

Word Bank

a. water

b. Seven

c. love

1. A sign of Baptism is ☐.

2. Sacraments are signs of God's ☐.

3. The Catholic Church has ☐ Sacraments.

B **Check Understanding** Fill in the circle beside the correct answer.

4. What special signs and actions did Jesus give us?

○ Commandments　　○ Sacraments

5. What do all Sacraments have?

○ bread　　○ words and actions

6. What did Jesus do for people?

○ hurt them　　○ healed them

7. What are the Sacraments?

○ celebrations　　○ stories

8. What Sacrament has the Body and Blood of Christ?

○ Eucharist　　○ Baptism

Go to **aliveinchrist.osv.com** for an interactive review.

© Our Sunday Visitor

FAMILY+FAITH
LIVING AND LEARNING TOGETHER

YOUR CHILD LEARNED >>>

This chapter identifies the Seven Sacraments as special signs and celebrations that Jesus gave his Church.

God's Word

 Read **John 14:20** to learn what Jesus says about being one with him and God the Father.

Catholics Believe

- The Church has Seven Sacraments. They are signs and celebrations that Jesus gave his Church.

- The Sacraments allow us to share in the life and work of God.

To learn more, go to the *Catechism of the Catholic Church* #1131–1134 at **usccb.org**.

People of Faith

This week, your child met Mary and learned a little about the Annunciation. Mary trusted the Holy Spirit, even when she didn't fully understand.

CHILDREN AT THIS AGE >>>

How They Understand the Sacraments As visible signs of invisible, spiritual realities, the Seven Sacraments are difficult for children in first grade to understand. Still, they are such a vital part of the life of the Church that we want children to be exposed to learning about the Sacraments very early. As time goes by, your child will understand more fully. In the meantime, you can explain that a Sacrament is something we can see that helps us understand something that we can't see. The people performing the visible sign and the community gathered work together with God making present the invisible, spiritual reality.

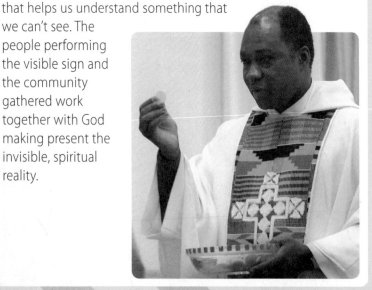

CONSIDER THIS >>>

What are some signs you recognize when your child is sick?

Is it flushed ears, or watery eyes? Or perhaps it is when he or she just wants to be held? We see these signs as indicators of something more. In the Seven Sacraments, we see signs that indicate something more—God's love and presence. "As we come to understand the Sacraments, it is important to recognize that the Sacraments have a visible and invisible reality, a reality open to all the human senses but grasped in its God-given depths with the eyes of faith" (*USCCA, p.168*).

LET'S TALK >>>

- At Mass, ask your child to point out some objects or actions that help people celebrate the Sacraments.

- Get out pictures from family Baptisms, First Communions, or weddings. Talk about the Sacraments that were celebrated on those days.

LET'S PRAY >>>

 Holy Mary, Mother of God, pray for us now and always. Amen.

 For a multimedia glossary of Catholic Faith Words, Sunday readings, seasonal and Saint resources, and chapter activities go to **aliveinchrist.osv.com**.

We Are Welcomed

 Let Us Pray

Leader: God, you have given us water to refresh us.

You made springs flow in valleys that wind among the mountains.

Based on Psalm 104:10

All: Thank you, God, for living water that gives us life. Amen.

 God's Word

"Go into the whole world and proclaim the gospel to every creature. Whoever believes and is baptized will be saved." Mark 16:15–16

 **What Do You Wonder?**

- What is being baptized like?
- When were you baptized?

Getting Started

In this chapter you will learn that grace is sharing in God's life and help. You will also learn that the Sacrament of Baptism brings new life in God and welcomes people into the Church family.

Use this chart to show what you know about the Sacrament of Baptism.

Check off some people or things you have seen during a Baptism.

People or Things I've Seen at Baptism

✓ Water		✓ Candle
✓ Godparents		✓ A priest
✓ A baby		✓ Holy oil
✓ Deacon		✓ Parents

Catholic Faith Words

Here are the vocabulary words for this chapter:

- Baptism
- grace
- godparents

Activity

Special Celebrations Draw a celebration that you have been a part of. Why was it special? Make sure to include the things you used to help you celebrate.

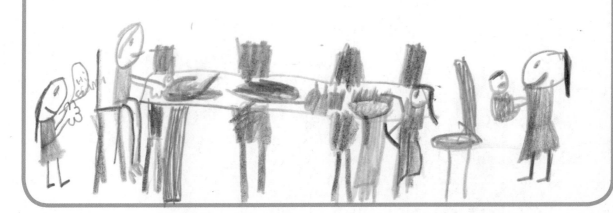

Welcome!

What Sacrament welcomes you into the Church?

Our Catholic Tradition

For more, go to page **364**

Baptism is the Sacrament that makes you a child of God and member of the Church. It is your welcome into the Church. God chooses you to be in the Church family.

With Baptism, the Holy Spirit comes. God makes you his own child. You receive a share in his life. God's life and love in you is called **grace**.

After Jesus went back to his Father in Heaven, the followers of Jesus welcomed everyone to be part of the Church.

God's Word

People Everywhere Believe

Philip traveled to different towns to tell others the Good News about Jesus. He shared Jesus' message and his love. In the name of Jesus, he even healed people who were sick. Many people began to believe in Jesus and were baptized. **Based on Acts 8:4–12**

Catholic Faith Words

Baptism the Sacrament in which a person is immersed in water or has water poured on him or her. Baptism takes away Original Sin and all personal sin, and makes a person a child of God and member of the Church.

grace God's gift of a share in his life and help

People who are baptized and who follow Jesus are called Christians. Baptism helps you do Jesus' work.

You can be kind to others and obey your parents. You can tell others about Jesus and his love. You can show others you care by sharing.

➜ **What are other ways children can do Jesus' work?**

 **Activity**

Think Write one way you can tell others about Jesus.

I, promise to

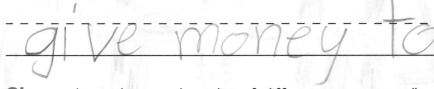
give money to the poor.

Share As a class, make a list of different ways to tell others about Jesus.

Becoming Church Members

What happens in Baptism?

1

Holy Water is poured over you three times while these words are prayed: "[Your name], I baptize you in the name of the Father, and of the Son, and of the Holy Spirit" **(Rite of Baptism)**.

2

The priest then says that you will remain a member of Christ forever and uses Sacred Chrism to make a cross on your head. This gesture is a sign that you are chosen by God to be a member of the Church.

3

You receive a white garment. It is a sign of your new life in Christ and your membership in the Church.

4

Your parents or godparents are given a lit candle. Light is a sign of Jesus. Jesus asks you to be like a light and show his love to others.

Your parents and **godparents** are also signs of God's love. Your parents chose your godparents to help you follow Jesus and live as a child of God. The whole community will help you follow Jesus. They will be examples to you and will help you learn about the Church.

Catholic Faith Words

godparents two people chosen by your parents to help you follow Jesus. They are usually present at your Baptism.

Activity

Match Game Draw lines to match the words and the pictures.

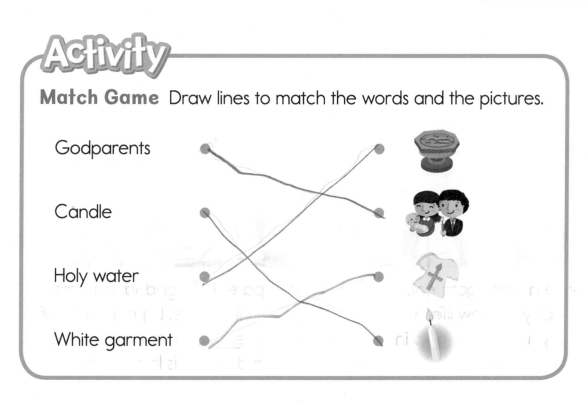

Godparents

Candle

Holy water

White garment

Our Catholic Life

How does your Baptism help you follow Jesus?

With Baptism, God called you to be a sign of his life and love. Here are some things God calls you to do.

Ways to Answer God's Call

Check off the things you can do this week to be a sign of God's life and love.

Show You Believe

Show that you believe in God the Father, God the Son, and God the Holy Spirit.

☐ Pray every day.

☐ Make the Sign of the Cross.

Be Like a Light

Be a light and share your goodness.

☐ Welcome everyone.

☐ Be a good example for younger children.

Live a New Life

Live a new life in the Church.

☐ Go to church with your family.

☐ Give up bad habits that lead to sin.

Love and Serve

Love and serve God.

☐ Do your chores cheerfully.

☐ Share what you have.

People of Faith

Saint Moses the Black, fourth century

Saint Moses was a robber when he was a young man. Many people were frightened of him because he was very tall and very mean and he became unhappy with his life. A monk told Moses about God and God's love for him. Moses was baptized and learned to love Jesus. Later he became a priest. He taught others about God's love and encouraged them to be baptized.

August 28

Discuss: Have you been at a Baptism? What did you see?

Learn more about Saint Moses the Black at **aliveinchrist.osv.com**

Activity

Baptism Memories Color the frame and the words. In the frame, draw or glue a picture of your Baptism.

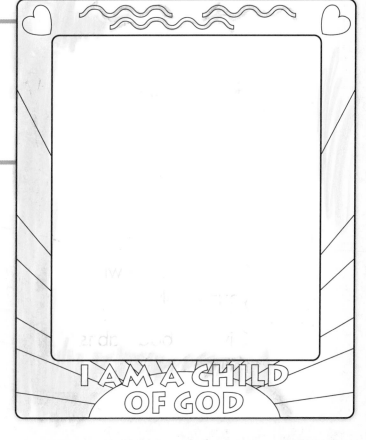

I AM A CHILD OF GOD

 **Let Us Pray**

Blessing Prayer

Gather and begin with the Sign of the Cross.

Leader: Glory be to the Father, and to the Son, and to the Holy Spirit:

All: as it was in the beginning, is now, and ever shall be, world without end. Amen.

Leader: Today we celebrate the gift of our Baptism. And so we remember that day by saying what we believe:

All: Sing "Yes, Lord, I Believe"

I believe in God the Father,
I believe in God the Son,
I believe in the Holy Spirit,
And the strength that makes us one.
I believe that Mother Mary
Is the Mother of God's Son.
I believe, I do believe.

Chapter 18 Review

A **Work with Words** Circle the correct answer.

1. ____ makes a person a child of God and member of the Church.

   Working   Baptism

2. Your ____ were chosen by your parents to help you follow Jesus.

   godparents   grandparents

3. Sharing in God's life and help is called ____.

   creation   grace

B **Check Understanding** Number the steps of Baptism in order from 1–4.

4. ☐ You receive a lit candle.

   ☐ Your head is marked with Sacred Chrism.

   ☐ Water is poured over you three times.

   ☐ You are given a white garment.

Go to aliveinchrist.osv.com for an interactive review.

FAMILY+FAITH
LIVING AND LEARNING TOGETHER

YOUR CHILD LEARNED >>>

This chapter examines the signs and symbols of Baptism and explains that baptized people are children of God and members of the Church.

God's Word

 Read **Mark 16:15–16** to learn about who is saved by Jesus Christ.

Catholics Believe

- Grace is God's gift of a share in his life and help.
- Baptism is the Sacrament in which a person is immersed in water or has water poured on him or her. Baptism brings new life in God and makes the person a member of the Church.

To learn more, go to the *Catechism of the Catholic Church* #1277–1282 at **usccb.org**.

People of Faith

This week, your child met Saint Moses the Black, a former robber in what is now Egypt, who became a dedicated monk and priest.

CHILDREN AT THIS AGE >>>

How They Understand Baptism First-grade children are very curious about Baptisms. There is always excitement when children this age are permitted to come near the baptismal font as someone is being baptized. They are intrigued by the pouring of the water. They are also able to understand that through the ritual actions and words of the rite, something deeper is occurring. Talk about your memories of your child's Baptism, and show him or her photos from that special day.

CONSIDER THIS >>>

How true is it for you that when you married your spouse you married his/her family?

One of the great joys and challenges of the first year of marriage is realizing that you are part of an entire "other" family. You married one person, but got a whole family. In Baptism, when we enter into divine life, by becoming one with Christ, we also got a whole family—the Church. "A person is initiated into God's people not by physical birth, but by a spiritual birth through faith in Christ and Baptism" *(USCCA, p. 116).*

LET'S TALK >>>

- Ask your child to name some ways he or she welcomes people at home.
- Talk about some ways God has called you and name some things you've done to answer God's call.

LET'S PRAY >>>

 Dear Jesus, thank you for making us a part of your family through Baptism. Amen.

 For a multimedia glossary of Catholic Faith Words, Sunday readings, seasonal and Saint resources, and chapter activities go to **aliveinchrist.osv.com**.

A **Work with Words** Complete each sentence with the letter of the correct word or words from the Word Bank.

Word Bank

a. grace

b. Savior

c. Jesus

d. Baptism

e. Sacraments

1. The Resurrection is the name for

   [C] being raised from Death to

   new life.

2. Jesus is the [b].

3. [e] are special signs and celebrations

   that Jesus gave his Church.

4. [d] takes away sin and makes you a member

   of the Church.

5. [a] is a sharing in God's life and help.

B **Check Understanding** Circle the word or words that answers the question.

6. Who did God send to save people?

Mary   Mass   ~~Jesus~~

7. Why does Jesus give us the Sacraments?

~~To show love~~   To tell stories   To buy things

8. What does Baptism call you to be?

Good at sports   Tall   A sign of love

C **Make Connections** Write the words that mean a sign of God's love.

9. Sending Jesus to the world.

Draw a sign for the Sacraments listed below.

10. Baptism

11. Eucharist

12. Matrimony

Kingdom of God

Our Catholic Tradition

- Jesus is always with us in the Eucharist. (CCC, 1377)

- God wants us to be happy with him forever, in this world and in Heaven. (CCC, 1023)

- All people who follow Jesus and obey God's laws will eventually be with God in Heaven forever. (CCC, 1053, 1054)

- We have an important job on Earth to be a sign of God's Kingdom to others. (CCC, 546)

Our Catholic Life

- At Mass we all have a part in the things we say and do to worship God. (CCC, 1348)

- We miss someone who has died. We trust that they will be with God forever in Heaven and that we remain united to them in special ways. (CCC, 1689)

- God asks us to work for his Kingdom by showing justice, love, and peace to others. (CCC, 2046)

How do we know God's love—every day, at Mass, and in Heaven?

We Give Thanks

Let Us Pray

Leader: God, we worship you with joy.

"Let us come before him with a song
of praise,
joyfully sing out our psalms."
Psalm 95:2

All: God, we worship you with joy. Amen.

God's Word

"While they were eating, Jesus took bread, said the blessing, broke it, and giving it to his disciples said, 'Take and eat; this is my body.' Then he took a cup, gave thanks, and gave it to [his disciples] saying, 'Drink from it, all of you, for this is my blood of the covenant, which shall be shed on behalf of many for the forgiveness of sins.'" Matthew 26:26–28

? What Do You Wonder?

- Who did Jesus invite to his meal?
- Why is eating a meal with people we love so important?

Getting Started

Catholic Faith Words

Here are the vocabulary words for this chapter:

- Last Supper
- Eucharist
- Mass
- Holy Communion

In this chapter you will learn that the Church family celebrates God's love in a special way at Mass, when Jesus gives himself to us in the Eucharist. In the Mass we hear God's Word, give thanks for his gifts, and recieve Jesus in Holy Communion.

Use the table below to show what you know about how we celebrate Mass.

 Check off the things you have seen, heard, or done during Mass.

Ways We Celebrate

 We sing to give God praise and thanks.

 We make the Sign of the Cross.

 The priest and altar servers walk in together as Mass begins.

 We listen to God's Word read from the Bible.

 People walk up to receive the gift of Jesus in Holy Communion.

 We give each other the sign of peace.

Activity

Special Meals Look at the pictures and write what you think the families are celebrating during these special meals.

Chirstmas   Easter

Draw a special meal that you have been a part of.

The Eucharist

Who is present in the Eucharist?

At Mass, the Church remembers an important night with Jesus. He shared a special meal with his followers. This meal is called the **Last Supper**.

Underline what Jesus said during the Last Supper.

 God's Word

The Last Supper

On the night before he died, Jesus shared a special meal with his friends.

He took the bread, gave thanks and broke it, and said, "This is my body that is for you. Do this in remembrance of me."

Jesus took the cup and said, "This cup is the new covenant in my blood. Do this, as often as you drink it, in remembrance of me."

Based on 1 Corinthians 11:23–25

➤ **When do you hear these words?**

Giving Thanks

At Mass, we celebrate the Sacrament of the **Eucharist**. The word Eucharist means thanksgiving. Catholics are thankful for all of God the Father's gifts, most especially his Son. We are thankful that Jesus is truly present in the Eucharist. Mass is celebrated in our parish church and in Catholic churches all over the world!

Activity

Think Look at the picture on this page.

Share As a class, talk about what is happening in the picture.

© Our Sunday Visitor

Catholic Faith Words

Last Supper the meal Jesus shared with his disciples the night before he died. At the Last Supper, Jesus gave himself in the Eucharist.

Eucharist the Sacrament in which Jesus shares himself, and the bread and wine become his Body and Blood

During Mass

What do we celebrate at Mass?

Our Catholic Tradition
For more, go to page 370

Many families celebrate their love for God with stories, songs, gifts, and food.

At **Mass**, the Church gathers to worship God. The Mass includes readings from the Bible, remembering that Jesus gave his life for us, and receiving **Holy Communion**—Jesus' Body and Blood in the celebration of the Eucharist

➜ **What do you know about the Mass?**

© Our Sunday Visitor

Catholic Faith Words

Mass the gathering of Catholics to worship God. It includes readings from the Bible and the celebration of Holy Communion.

Holy Communion receiving Jesus' Body and Blood in the celebration of the Eucharist

1 You gather to sing and pray.

2 You listen to readings from the Bible.

Activity

Word Scramble Unscramble the letters to find words that tell what the Church does during Mass.

ngsi　　　s i n g

ayrp　　　p r a y

ksthan　　t h a n k s

3 The bread and the wine become the Body and Blood of Jesus.

4 Those who are old enough receive Jesus in Holy Communion.

© Our Sunday Visitor

Our Catholic Life

What do you see and do at Mass?

When you go to Mass, you see many people and things. You do many things, too.

➤ **What else have you seen or done at Mass?**

Circle the people and things you have seen or the things you have done at Mass.

At Mass

People You Might See	Things You Might See	Things You Might Do
• Priest	• Altar	• Make the Sign of the Cross
• Altar server	• Candles	• Sing and pray
• Song leader	• Book of Gospels	• Share a sign of peace
• Reader	• Chalice	• Receive Holy Communion
• Extraordinary Minister of Holy Communion	• Crucifix	

People of Faith

Pope Saint John XXIII
(Angelo Roncalli), 1881–1963

Pope John XXIII was known for his kindness and generosity. He was named Pope when he was much older. He hadn't expected it. Many were surprised when he called together a special council of Bishops to talk about important things, like how Catholics worship at Mass and live in the world. Many people called him "Good Pope John."

October 11

Discuss: What can you tell others about the Mass?

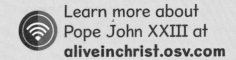

Learn more about Pope John XXIII at **aliveinchrist.osv.com**

Activity

Draw Yourself at Mass Draw a picture of yourself and your family at Mass.

 **Let Us Pray**

Reflection Prayer

Gather and begin with the Sign of the Cross.

Leader: Jesus, we ask you to open our hearts
as we remember once again
the gift of your life and love in
Holy Communion.

Leader: A reading about the Last Supper
from the Bible.

Read the adaptation of
1 Corinthians 11:23–25. (See page 306.)

The word of the Lord.

All: Thanks be to God.

Leader: Lead the reflection prayer.

All: Pray the Glory Be together.
(See page 378.)

Chapter 19 Review

A **Work with Words** Fill in the blank with the letter of the correct word or words from the Word Bank.

Word Bank

a. Eucharist

b. Last Supper

c. Bible

d. Holy Communion

e. Mass

1. Jesus shared the **b** with his disciples the night before he died.

2. Church members receive Jesus in **d**.

3. The **e** is the gathering of Catholics to worship God.

4. Jesus shares himself in the Sacrament of the **a**.

5. You hear readings from the **b** at Mass.

B **Check Understanding** Circle the correct answer.

6. The word Eucharist means ____.

   (thanksgiving)   Bible

7. The ____ become the Body and Blood of Christ.

   holy water   (bread and wine)

Go to **aliveinchrist.osv.com** for an interactive review.

© Our Sunday Visitor

FAMILY+FAITH
LIVING AND LEARNING TOGETHER

YOUR CHILD LEARNED >>>

This chapter identifies the Mass as the Sacrament of the Eucharist, the Church's great celebration of praise and thanksgiving.

God's Word

 Read **Matthew 26:26–28** to learn how Jesus shared a meal with his friends.

Catholics Believe

- At Mass, we gather to worship God by reading from the Bible, giving thanks, and receiving Holy Communion.

- Jesus shares his Body and Blood with us in the Eucharist.

To learn more, go to the *Catechism of the Catholic Church* #1322–1327 at **usccb.org**.

People of Faith

This week, your child met Pope Saint John XXIII. He helped change the way Catholics all over the world celebrate the Mass.

CHILDREN AT THIS AGE >>>

How They Understand the Mass Some children in first grade have difficulty engaging in the Mass, perhaps because the language of the Mass, hymns, and homily often feel very much directed toward the adults in the parish. Helping your child become familiar with what happens at Mass, the words that are said and their meanings can help him or her to begin to decode what may otherwise feel like a very adult event. At the same time, we need to retain our sense of awe and mystery at the miracle of God's love unfolding before us.

CONSIDER THIS >>>

Why is it so important to gather together for meals?

Eating together helps us grow and gain a greater sense of belonging and a true sense of ourselves. Those same human longings guide us to Mass. Here we are strengthened in our identity as members of the Body of Christ and grow in deeper communion with one another. "Holy Communion increases our union with Christ. Just as bodily food sustains our physical life, so Holy Communion nourishes our spiritual life. This Communion moves us away from sin, strengthening our moral resolve to avoid evil and turn ever more powerfully toward God" (*USCCA, p. 223*).

LET'S TALK >>>

- Ask your child to recall some things that he or she does during Mass.

- Talk about your favorite part of the Mass and how you first became familiar with what happens at Mass.

LET'S PRAY >>>

 Dear God, help our family always give thanks for the good things you have done for us and to share those stories with others. Amen.

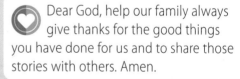 For a multimedia glossary of Catholic Faith Words, Sunday readings, seasonal and Saint resources, and chapter activities go to **aliveinchrist.osv.com**.

Forever with God

 Let Us Pray

Leader: God, guide us and love us every day.

"LORD, show me your way;
lead me on a level path
because of my enemies."
Psalm 27:11

All: God, guide us and love us every day. Amen.

✝ God's Word

Some people asked Jesus when God's Kingdom would come. Jesus answered, "The coming of the kingdom of God cannot be observed, and no one will announce, 'Look, here it is,' or, 'There it is.' For behold the kingdom of God is among you." Based on Luke 17:20–21

? What Do You Wonder?

- What does God's Kingdom look like?

- When will you share God's love with someone today?

Getting Started

© Our Sunday Visitor

Catholic Faith Words

Here is the vocabulary word for this chapter:

- Heaven

In this chapter you will learn that everyone who accepts God's gift of grace by having faith in him and following Jesus will be happy with God forever.

In the boxes below show what you know about Heaven.

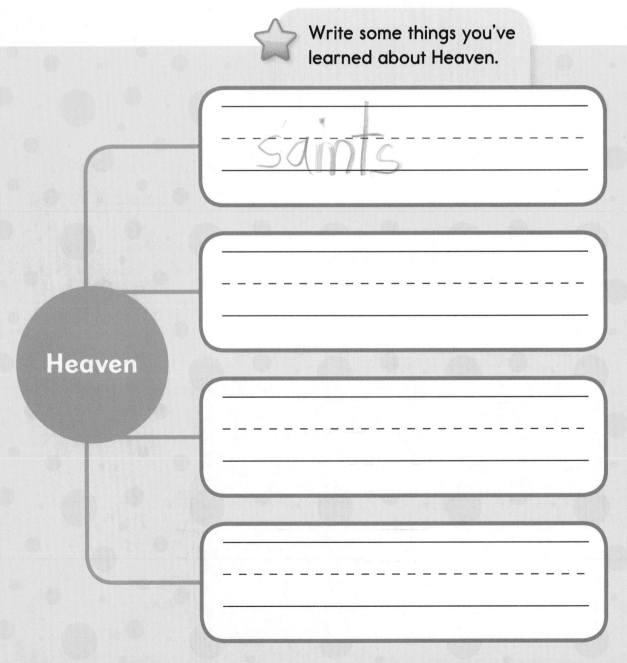

Write some things you've learned about Heaven.

saints

Heaven

Activity

Life with God Write about some of the ways that God takes care of you and helps you to be happy.

God takes care of me and helps me to be happy at home by:

_____

_____

_____

_____

_____

_____

_____

God takes care of me and helps me to be happy at school by:

_____

_____

_____

_____

_____

_____

_____

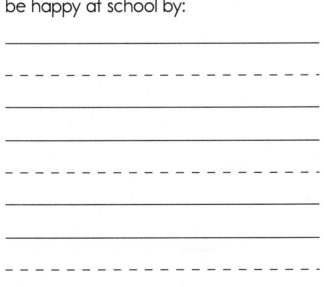

Life Forever with God

What is Heaven?

Like plants and animals, people have life cycles. People are born, they live, and then they die. Listen to the promise Jesus made about life after death.

© Our Sunday Visitor

Catholic Faith Words

Heaven the full joy of living with God forever

📖 God's Word

Together Always

Jesus told his followers, "Do not let your hearts be troubled. You have faith in God; have faith also in me. In my Father's house there are many dwelling spaces. If there were not, would I have told you that I'm going to prepare a place for you?"

Based on John 14:1–2

➜ What do you think it is like with God the Father?

Happiness Forever

Jesus said that he will come back to bring his followers to his Father's house. Jesus said they will have joy that will never end. After death, Jesus' followers can have new life with God. They can be full of happiness. **Heaven** is the full joy of living with God forever.

Think Draw some things that make you happy here on Earth.

Share As a class, talk about what might make you happy in Heaven.

Happy Forever

What do you need to do to be happy with God forever?

The Holy Trinity lives in love forever. All holy people who have died are living in love and happiness forever with the Holy Trinity.

St. Joan of Arc

St. Francis of Assisi

St. Jude

St. Martin de Porres

The Way to Heaven

God wants everyone to be happy forever, even after they die. Everyone is invited. Everyone who accepts God's gift of grace by having faith and following Jesus will one day be in Heaven with God.

St. Bernadette

Draw someone in your family who has helped you learn more about following Jesus.

Activity

Doing What Jesus Says In the Bible, Jesus tells us how to live. Write one action that Jesus wants us to do.

Atend church

Our Catholic Life

What do we do when someone dies?

When someone we love dies, we are sad. We know that we will miss the person. Since we are followers of Jesus, we know that death is not really the end. Even though we miss the person now, we know we will meet him or her again in Heaven.

Our Catholic Tradition

For more, go to page **369**

Here are some things the followers of Jesus do when someone dies.

Place a check mark next to one thing you or someone in your family has done.

When Someone Dies

 We let ourselves feel sad. We share how we feel with God and with other people we love.

 We gather for Mass. We thank God for giving us this person to be in our lives.

 We share happy memories with family and friends. We tell stories about our loved one.

 We ask God to take care of the person who has died. We ask God to welcome him or her to Heaven.

© Our Sunday Visitor

People of Faith

Saint Emily de Vialar, 1797–1856

Saint Emily was born in France. When she was fifteen, her mother died. She took care of her father's house. She devoted her life to prayer. After inheriting some money, she cared for children who were sick and poor. Saint Emily taught the children that we should always love each other. She also taught them that Jesus wants us to be happy and live with God forever in Heaven.

June 17

Discuss: What makes you happy?

Learn more about Saint Emily at **aliveinchrist.osv.com**

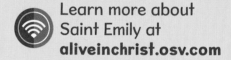

Say a Prayer Do you know someone who has died? This week, say a special prayer for that person.

Dear God,

Please take care of all those who have died,

especially _great granpa Patrik._

Amen.

 **Let Us Pray**

Prayer for the Dead

Gather and begin with the Sign of the Cross.

Leader: Those who have died as friends of God are part of our Church family. We pray for them. We ask them to pray for us, too.

Side 1: Lord, our God, we remember those who have died.

Side 2: Bring them home to be with you forever.

Side 1: Gather us all together into your Kingdom.

Side 2: There we will be happy forever with the Virgin Mary, Mother of God and our Mother.

All: There all the friends of the Lord Jesus will sing a song of joy.

From the *Eucharistic Prayer II for Children*

 Sing "Around Your Throne"

We gather around your throne O God.
You are worthy of our praise.
With the saints and all the angels,
in one voice we worship you.
Holy (Holy)
Holy (Holy)
Holy….. are you!

© 2010, Banner Kidd. Published by Our Sunday Visitor.

A **Work with Words** Complete each sentence.

1. God wants everyone to be _____.

2. Jesus said that after death you can _____

   have new _____.

3. You can be happy with God when you _____

   _____ Jesus.

4. You can have the full joy of living with God _____

   forever in _____.

Word Bank

follow

life

Heaven

happy

B **Check Understanding** Put the events in order.

5. ☐ We have life forever with God.

6. ☐ We die.

7. ☐ We are born.

8. ☐ We live.

 Go to **aliveinchrist.osv.com** for an interactive review.

© Our Sunday Visitor

FAMILY+FAITH
LIVING AND LEARNING TOGETHER

YOUR CHILD LEARNED >>>

This chapter explains Heaven as the full joy of living with God forever. God wants everyone to live in love and happiness with him.

God's Word

 See **Luke 17:20–21** to read what Jesus said about the coming of the Kingdom of God.

Catholics Believe

- Jesus said those who die can have new life with him in Heaven.
- God invites all people to Heaven. All who follow Jesus and obey God's laws will go to Heaven.

To learn more, go to the *Catechism of the Catholic Church* #1023–1025 at **usccb.org**.

People of Faith

This week, your child met Saint Emily de Vialar. Saint Emily had a special love for sick children and taught them that Jesus wants them to be happy here and in Heaven.

CHILDREN AT THIS AGE >>>

How They Understand Life with God First-graders are still forming a concept of Heaven as they struggle with the idea that death is a permanent change and is different from sleeping. If your child has had a grandparent or another family member who died, he or she might have been told that the person "went to Heaven." Children this age tend to think of Heaven as a place somewhere way up in the sky. This can make them also think about life without a parent or caregiver. Because of this, they can be afraid of death and therefore afraid of Heaven. Eternal life, a difficult concept even for us as adults, is fairly incomprehensible for young children. Be careful how you talk to children about Heaven. Even if it sounds marvelous, they may be reluctant in wanting to go!

CONSIDER THIS >>>

What does forever mean to you?

As a child it may have been the time we waited for Christmas or a birthday. As a young adult we may focus on the seeming "forever" of things to come—marriage, family, retirement. The older we get, the more we realize that forever is more than this life. "Every time we attend a funeral vigil or Mass, view a deceased body at a wake, or pass by a cemetery, we are reminded of this simple and profound article of the Creed, the belief in the resurrection of the body. It is a sobering belief, because it reminds us of the judgment yet to come, and at the same time it is a joyful belief that heralds life everlasting with God" (*USCCA, p. 156*).

LET'S TALK >>>

- Ask your child about Jesus' promise to his followers.
- Talk about loved ones who have passed away and what living forever with God means to you.

LET'S PRAY >>>

 Saint Emily, pray for us that we may be happy here on Earth and in Heaven with Jesus. Amen.

For a multimedia glossary of Catholic Faith Words, Sunday readings, seasonal and Saint resources, and chapter activities go to **aliveinchrist.osv.com**.

God's Kingdom

 Let Us Pray

Leader: God, you teach us how to live every day.

"Your reign is a reign for all ages,
    your dominion for all generations.
The LORD is trustworthy in all his words,
    and loving in all his works." Psalm 145:13–14

All: God, guide us in working for your
    Kingdom. Amen.

🄳 **God's Word**

"You have been told...what the LORD requires of you: Only to do justice and to love goodness, and to walk humbly with your God." Micah 6:8

? What Do You Wonder?

- How do you do what is right?
- When do you bring peace to others?

Getting Started

In this chapter you will learn that when we are kind, share, play fair, and include others we are spreading peace and working with God to build his Kingdom.

Use the empty boxes below to show what you already know about peace.

© Our Sunday Visitor

Catholic Faith Words

Here is the vocabulary word for this chapter:

• peace

Write or draw some ways you can bring peace to others.

Activity

God's Kingdom Read each pair of scenarios. Place a check mark next to the one that is an example of spreading peace and caring for others.

 A group of friends are playing ball. Frank wants to join. He is told "No!" by the other children.

 A group of friends are playing ball. Kindly they all ask Frank to come play with them.

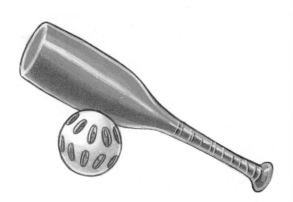

 After school, Lucy keeps all the video games to herself.

 When playing, the group plays together and everyone takes turns.

 At lunch, Alex calls someone mean names and begins to tease him about the food he has for lunch.

At lunch, Gigi drops her napkin and someone who has two napkins offers to share.

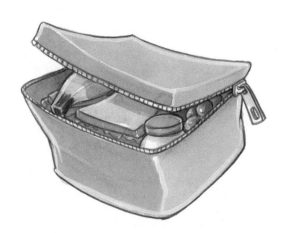

Love and Peace

How can you work together with God as he builds his Kingdom?

Our Catholic Tradition

For more, go to page **356**

Underline what Jesus taught us to pray for. Where do you hear these words?

God's Word in Scripture teaches us how to have true happiness. In Heaven, everyone is happy because they are with God. Everyone gets along and loves each other. Jesus taught us to pray that God's Kingdom would come "on earth as it is in Heaven."

When we celebrate God's goodness and treat others with love, we are working to bring peace as he builds his Kingdom.

- Jesus forgave people over and over again. Jesus brought peace.
- Jesus treated others as he would like to be treated. Jesus brought justice.
- Jesus fed people who were hungry. Jesus showed love.

The Kingdom Grows

When we love God and others and do even small things to show our love, we work with God to spread the Good News of his Kingdom.

Every day, God gives us many ways to make small, loving choices. The good things we do each day help God's Kingdom to grow.

➜ **How can you spread the Good News?**

God's Word

Starting Small

Jesus said that God's Kingdom is like a mustard seed. It is a very tiny seed that grows to be a very big tree. It becomes so big that birds can sit in its branches. **Based on Matthew 13:31–32**

Activity

Think Write one good thing that you do every day to help God's Kingdom grow.

_____

_ _

_____

Share with a classmate.

Living for the Kingdom

How can you help God's Kingdom grow?

When followers of Jesus act with **peace**, justice, and love, they help the Kingdom of God grow.

How can children work with God as he builds his Kingdom? How can they share God's love with others?

© Our Sunday Visitor

Catholic Faith Words

peace when things are calm and people get along with one another

1. Place a check mark next to the things that build up God's Kingdom.

2. Put an X next to the things that do not build up God's Kingdom.

Some quiet or shy children don't get picked as partners.

☐ Ignore the children who never get picked because they must not be good partners.

☐ Kindly ask one of them to be a partner. This is spreading peace.

Some children don't want to share.

☐ Keep your toys to yourself and don't share them with others.

☐ Share and give others what they need. This is acting with justice.

When the teacher isn't looking, some children are teasing and calling others names.

☐ Show care for others, even if it's hard. This is love.

☐ Join in the teasing so you don't get picked on next.

Activity

Make a Membership Card
Write your name in the space below. Talk about ways you can help God's Kingdom grow.

MEMBERSHIP CARD

God's Kingdom

You !
_____
MEMBER

Expiration Date: Never

_____

- -

_____

Our Catholic Life

How can you live in the Kingdom of God?

God's Kingdom grows whenever people show justice, love, and peace. Here are some ways you can live in and show others God's Kingdom.

In the empty puzzle piece, draw one way you live in God's Kingdom.

Bring justice

- Play fair.
- Share what you have with others.
- Don't leave anyone out.
- Help people get the food and clothing they need.

Bring love

- Show family members and friends that you care.
- Be happy when good things happen to others.
- Help those who are feeling hurt or lonely.
- Don't gossip or call people mean names.

Bring peace

- Be patient.
- Try to settle an argument so everyone wins.
- Don't always try to get your way.
- Be the first to say "I'm sorry" and "I forgive you."

People of Faith

Saint Pedro Calungsod, 1654–1672

Saint Pedro Calungsod was born in the Philippines. At fourteen he became a lay missionary. Pedro was a painter, singer, and catechist as he worked with the Jesuit missionaries. His greatest desire was to spread Jesus' message of love. He died while protecting a priest from men who hated Christianity. Pedro is the patron Saint of Filipino children.

April 2

Discuss: How can you use your talents to spread Jesus' message of love?

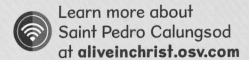

Learn more about Saint Pedro Calungsod at **aliveinchrist.osv.com**

Activity

Imagine Draw a picture of what the world would be like if everyone worked together to help build God's Kingdom.

 **Let Us Pray**

Asking Prayer

Gather and begin with the Sign of the Cross.

Leader: God, we want to do your will.

All: Help us bring peace.

Leader: God the Father, we want to do your will.

All: Help us bring justice.

Leader: God, we want to do your will.

All: Help us bring love.

 Sing "Right and Just"

It is right—the proper thing to do.
It is just—giving God what's due.
When we come to praise our God,
It is right and just.

A **Work with Words** Fill in the blank with the correct word from the Word Bank.

Word Bank

love

peace

justice

1. When you settle problems with kindness, you bring _____.

2. When you care, even if it's hard, you bring _____.

3. When you give God what he deserves and give others what they need, you bring _____.

B **Check Understanding** Put an X by things you can do to help God's Kingdom grow.

4. ☐ love your parents

5. ☐ be a good friend

6. ☐ tease

7. ☐ pray

8. ☐ fight

9. ☐ help others

Go to **aliveinchrist.osv.com** for an interactive review.

FAMILY+FAITH
LIVING AND LEARNING TOGETHER

YOUR CHILD LEARNED >>>

This chapter explores bringing happiness to others and helping God's Kingdom grow.

God's Word

 Read **Micah 6:8** to see how God wants us to live so that we can be with him in Heaven.

Catholics Believe

- Justice, love, and peace are signs of God's Kingdom.
- Catholics work here and now with God to help his Kingdom continue to grow.

To learn more, go to the *Catechism of the Catholic Church* #2816–2821 at **usccb.org**.

People of Faith

This week, your child met Saint Pedro Calungsod, a teenage Filipino catechist who was martyred for the faith.

CHILDREN AT THIS AGE >>>

How They Understand God's Kingdom First-grade children are familiar with stories, such as fairy tales, that involve kings and kingdoms, and they might think of Jesus' references to the Father's Kingdom in these terms. You can help your child understand that Christians cooperate with God to help God's Kingdom grow "on earth as it is in Heaven." We will live forever with God in his Kingdom in Heaven, but we also actively work to help God's Kingdom grow by showing love to one another.

CONSIDER THIS >>>

Without using words, how do we show our children that we love them?

Actions speak louder than words. Making a favorite meal, catching a ball, or wiping away tears as you put on a bandage are all signs of your love. We make God's life and love present with our words, attitudes, and actions—we manifest God's Kingdom. "The proclamation of the Kingdom of God was fundamental to Jesus' preaching. The Kingdom of God is his presence among human beings calling them to a new way of life as individuals and as a community… It is the Good News that results in love, justice and mercy for the whole world" (*USCCA, p. 79*).

LET'S TALK >>>

- Ask your child what small things he or she can do to help God's Kingdom grow.
- Talk about people who bring peace or share God's love in their daily lives.

LET'S PRAY >>>

 Saint Pedro, pray for us that we may live justice, love, and peace in our family today. Amen.

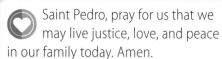 For a multimedia glossary of Catholic Faith Words, Sunday readings, seasonal and Saint resources, and chapter activities go to **aliveinchrist.osv.com**.

A **Work with Words** Fill in the blanks with the correct word or words from the Word Bank.

Word Bank

Heaven

Last Supper

peace

Jesus

everyone

1. Jesus shared the _____ _____ _____ with his disciples the night before he died.

2. At Mass, the bread and wine become _____ the Body and Blood of _____.

3. _____ is the full joy of living with God forever.

4. God wants _____ to be happy with him.

5. Jesus asks his followers to act with _____ _____.

B **Check Understanding** Draw a line to match the words in Column A with the definition in Column B.

Column A	Column B
6. Eucharist	receiving Jesus' Body and Blood
7. Holy Communion	the Church remembers this meal at Mass
8. God's Kingdom	Sacrament celebrated at Mass
9. Book of Gospels and Chalice	living in peace, love, and justice
10. The Last Supper	things you see used at Mass

C **Make Connections** Draw a picture of how you can make others happy.

11.

Life and Dignity

We read in the Bible that God knew us before we were even born: "Before I formed you...I knew you" (Jeremiah 1:5). God created each one of us. He has a plan for our lives. He knows what he made us to be.

Because God made each person, we should be kind and fair to everyone and take care of the bodies and minds God gave us, using them for good.

God wants us to be nice to others, and talk about problems instead of fighting. If someone else is being mean, we should speak up, and get help if necessary. We should help to protect others because every life is important to God.

The Gift of Life

People live in many different countries. They speak different languages. They have different colors of skin, hair, and eyes.

All people are the same in one important way. God made each one of us. God gave us the gift of his own life and love. God wants us to respect his life in others.

>> **What can you do to take care of other people?**

Learn About Others

You can learn a lot from people who are different from you. Answer the questions below.

1. What could you learn from someone who comes from another country?

_____

- -

_____

2. What could you learn from someone who has trouble seeing or hearing?

_____

- -

_____

Call to Community

God gives us families and communities because he knows it would not be good for us to live our lives alone. In fact, the Bible says that this is why God created Eve to be a companion and friend to Adam. (See Genesis 2:18.)

The Church teaches that God gives us families to help us learn who God is and how to love one another. Our parish community also helps us to learn about God. In families and in parish communities, we work together to take care of one another and to become the people God made us to be.

Planting a community garden is one way we can help take care of each other.

You Are Needed

What is a family without family members? What is a community without people? What is a parish without parishioners? Every group must have members. No group can continue to live and grow unless its members work together.

Your family, your parish, and your community would not be the same without you. You are needed. You can use the gifts God gave you to help in many groups in your community.

≫ **How do you participate in your family?**

Draw a Picture

Draw one way you take part in your community.

Rights and Responsibilities

Because God made every person, everyone has rights and responsibilities. Rights are the freedoms or things every person needs and should have. Responsibilities are our duties, or the things we must do.

Jesus said, "You shall love your neighbor as yourself" (Mark 12:31). Following this command means making sure everyone's rights are protected. We also have a responsibility to treat others well and work together for the good of everyone.

Living in Harmony

Have you ever heard a choir sing? Some people sing high notes, some sing low notes. When they sing together, they make harmony, a blend of beautiful sounds.

Every person has rights, things that he or she can do freely. Every person must also protect the rights of others. When everyone's rights are protected, we live in peace. We make the beautiful harmony of God's Kingdom.

≫ **What are some things that keep people from living in harmony?**

Check Your Understanding

Rights and responsibilities are not the same thing. Draw a line from the rights in Column B to the word "Rights" in column A. Do the same for responsibilities.

Column A	Column B
Rights	food
	doing homework
	shelter
Responsibilities	brushing teeth
	chores
	education

Option for the Poor

In Scripture, Jesus says that whatever we have done for people who are poor or needy, we have also done for him. (See Matthew 25:40.) We should treat people the same way we would treat Jesus himself. When people need food, drink, clothing, housing, or medical care, or when they are lonely, we should try extra hard to help.

Saint Rose of Lima said, "When we serve the poor and the sick, we serve Jesus." Our Church teaches that we should have special love and care for those who are poor and put their needs first. When we do this, God will bless us.

People in Need

One day Jesus was teaching a big crowd about God's love. Late in the afternoon, people started getting hungry, but they had no food. Jesus' disciples weren't sure what to do.

Jesus asked who had food. One boy was willing to share his five small loaves of bread and two fish. Jesus blessed the food. There were baskets of leftovers! (See John 6:1-13.)

We are called to be like Jesus and the boy. We should try to share what we have and give to others.

≫ **What do the people in your community need?**

Write a Response

Read the words and write something you could do to help.

1. A friend is feeling lonely. What can you do?

_____

_ _

_____

2. A new neighbor has no friends. What can you do?

_____

_ _

_____

The Dignity of Work

The different jobs people have help them earn money to buy food and other things they need to live. Jobs also allow people to work together with God and his creation. Work is part of God's plan for people, and everyone should work, either in or outside the home.

All adults should be able to have a job if they want one. Scripture teaches that workers should be treated fairly by their bosses. (See Deuteronomy 24:14.) They should be given fair pay for their work. (See Leviticus 19:13 and Deuteronomy 24:15.) If workers are unhappy, they should be able to work things out with their bosses.

Respect for Workers

People work in all kinds of jobs. People work to earn money and to use the gifts and talents God gave them.

Some workers do not earn enough money. Some workers become ill or injured and cannot work at all. The Church teaches that work and workers should be treated well. It should not matter who the workers are or what they do.

> **What does it mean to show respect for workers?**

True For You

You are a worker, too.

Read each sentence. If it is true for you, circle the happy face. If it is not, circle the sad face. If it is true sometimes, and you need to do better, circle the question mark.

1. I do my best school work.

2. I do my chores as soon as I am asked.

3. I am proud of the work I do.

4. I thank my family for the work they do.

Human Solidarity

People around the world are different in many ways. Our hair, eyes, and skin are many different colors. There are people who are rich, people who are poor, and people who are in-between.

But one way we are all alike is that God made us. We are one human family. (See Galatians 3:28.) God calls everyone to be his children. Because God made everyone, we should treat everyone with love, kindness, and fairness. In the Beatitudes, Jesus says, "Blessed are the peacemakers" (Matthew 5:9). Treating others fairly will help us to live in peace with one another.

One Big Neighborhood

Who are your neighbors? People who live close to you are neighbors. So are the people who live in your city or town.

Jesus taught that all people are our neighbors. Neighbors can live close by or far away. All humans are part of God's family.

Families and neighbors share good times and bad times. It is important for us to love our neighbors and treat them well.

≫ **How can you get to know your neighbors around the world?**

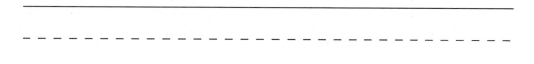

Solve the Puzzle

What can you do to help your neighbors? Circle the correct letter in each sentence and write them down to find one thing you can do for your neighbors.

1. Circle the letter that is in L O T but not in G O T.

2. Circle the letter that is in T O N but not in T A N.

3. Circle the letter that is in V A N but not in M A N.

4. Circle the letter that is in B E T but not in B I T.

_____

- -

_____

Care for Creation

God created the whole world—the Earth and sky, the mountains and deserts, and all of the plants, animals, and people. When God made these things, he called them "very good" (Genesis 1:31). God put people in charge of the fish, the birds, and all living things. (See Genesis 1:28.) God wants us to enjoy and take care of everything he has made.

Our Church teaches us that God gave us the plants and animals for the good of all people. We need to work to take care of the plants and animals and the places where they live, so everyone can enjoy them now and in the future.

Be My Helpers

You can be a good helper. You can help your family at home. You can help your teacher at school.

God asks you to be his helper, too. You can help take care of the gifts of God's creation. You can help by planting flowers and vegetables. You can feed wild birds. You can take care of your pets. You can also help keep parks and playgrounds clean.

≫ **Why should you take care of creation?**

Be a Good Helper

Draw yourself working to care for God's creation. What are some things you can do to help take care of the gifts of God's creation?

The Bible

The Bible is God's Word to his People. It is one great book, made up of many small books. The word Bible means "books." Another name for the Bible is Scripture, which means "writing." The Bible has two parts: the Old Testament and the New Testament.

The Old Testament

The Old Testament is the first part of the Bible and also the largest. It tells about God and his People before the coming of Jesus.

The New Testament

The second part of the Bible tells about the life and teaching of Jesus, his first followers, and the early Church. The New Testament contains four main sections: the Gospels, Acts of the Apostles, the Epistles, and the Book of Revelation.

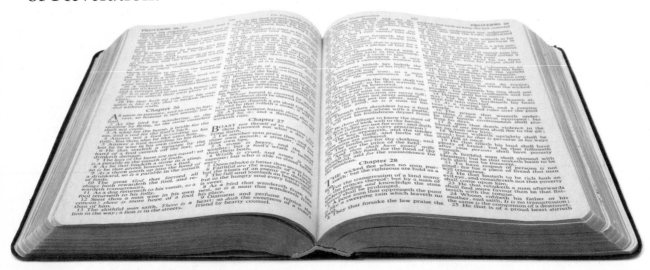

The Gospels

The first section of the New Testament is the Gospels. The word gospel means "Good News." The Gospels contain stories about Jesus. They tell us about his words, actions, teachings and miracles. There are four Gospels:

- Matthew
- Mark
- Luke
- John

Parables

Some special stories told by Jesus are called parables. Parables are short stories about everyday life that help people better understand a truth or mystery about God. Jesus told parables like the Good Shepherd, the Good Samaritan, and the King's Banquet to help others better understand how much God loves all people. Through his stories Jesus showed them that God wants everyone to be happy with him forever.

The Holy Trinity

The Holy Trinity is God the Father, God the Son, and God the Holy Spirit— three Divine Persons in one God.

- God the Father is the Creator of all that is.

- Jesus Christ is the Son of God and our Savior.

- God the Holy Spirit is God's gift of love to the Church.

When you make the Sign of the Cross and say, "In the name of the Father, and of the Son, and of the Holy Spirit," you are showing your belief in the Holy Trinity.

The Creed

The creed tells the faith of the Church. It brings together the Church's most important beliefs about the Holy Trinity and our Catholic faith.

The Apostles' Creed

This Creed is a summary of the Apostles' beliefs. We sometimes profess it at Mass during the Easter season and in Masses with children.

I believe in God,
the Father almighty,
Creator of heaven and earth,
and in Jesus Christ, his only Son,
  our Lord,

At the words that follow, up to and including the Virgin Mary, all bow.

who was conceived by the
  Holy Spirit,
born of the Virgin Mary,
suffered under Pontius Pilate,
was crucified, died and was
  buried;
he descended into hell;
on the third day he rose again
  from the dead;

he ascended into heaven,
and is seated at the right hand
  of God the Father almighty;
from there he will come to
  judge the living and the dead.

I believe in the Holy Spirit,
the holy catholic Church,
the communion of saints,
the forgiveness of sins,
the resurrection of the body,
and life everlasting. Amen.

The Church

The Church is the community of baptized people who believe in God and follow Jesus. The Church gathers to worship and praise God, especially at the celebration of the Mass.

Each member of the Church has been baptized and welcomed into God's family. Catholics have a mission to share God's message of love with others.

In order to carry out this mission, we receive the gift of the Holy Spirit. Jesus' followers received the Holy Spirit at Pentecost.

The Holy Spirit gave each of the disciples the courage to spread the Good News of Jesus to other people. The Holy Spirit also makes you strong.

Mary, the Mother of God

Mary is the Mother of God. She is also the Mother of the Church. Mary is a very special Saint. All her life, Mary said "yes" to the things God asked of her.

At the Annunciation the Angel Gabriel came to Mary to tell her she was going to give birth to the Savior, whom she should call Jesus. Because Mary said "yes," all people have been saved from the power of sin and everlasting death.

Mary is our great role model in the Church. The People of God often ask Mary to pray for them so that they have the courage to say "yes" to God, especially when it is difficult.

Honoring Mary

The Church honors Mary in many special ways. Special prayers, such as the Rosary, are said. Feast days, such as Our Lady of Guadalupe, are celebrated. We honor Mary at all times, but especially on her feast days. These prayers and feasts remind people that Mary was willing to serve God.

Many countries celebrate Mary in different ways. You can read about a few of these ways on the next page.

Our Lady of Guadalupe

In Mexico, Latin America, and the United States, the people honor Our Lady of Guadalupe. She appeared to Juan Diego on his way to Mass. A church was built on that site. Pope Saint John Paul II named Our Lady of Guadalupe the Patroness of the Americas.

Our Lady of Czestochowa

In Poland, the people honor the image of Our Lady of Czestochowa. Pope Saint John Paul II had a special devotion to this image of Mary, who is named queen of Poland. He visited her shrine just after becoming Pope in 1979.

Our Lady of Lourdes

In France, people honor Our Lady of Lourdes. Mary appeared to a young peasant girl named Bernadette. A spring of water flows at that spot. To this day it has healing power. People from all over visit the site.

The Seven Sacraments

The Sacraments are special signs and celebrations that Jesus gave his Church. They allow us to share in God's life and work.

Baptism

Baptism frees you of sin and makes you a child of God and member of the Church.

Confirmation

Confirmation seals us with the gift of the Holy Spirit and celebrates his help.

Eucharist

Jesus shares his life with us in the bread and wine that become his Body and Blood.

© Our Sunday Visitor

Penance and Reconciliation

You say you are sorry. Through the words and actions of the priest, God forgives your sins and strengthens you to live as he wants.

Anointing of the Sick

In the Anointing of the Sick, a priest blesses the very sick with holy oil. God gives comfort and peace.

Holy Orders

In Holy Orders God blesses men to be bishops, priests, and deacons who lead and serve the Church.

Matrimony

In Marriage, God blesses a baptized man and a baptized woman to live in love. Married love is the heart of a family.

Special Things in Church

Altar

The altar is the table at the front of the church that is used to celebrate the Mass.

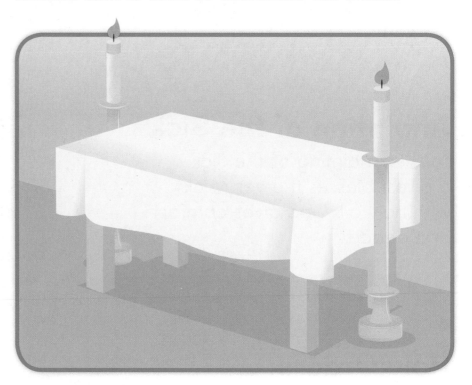

Tabernacle

The Tabernacle is a special place in the church where the Body of Christ, the Blessed Sacrament, is kept after Mass.

Vestments

The priest wears special clothing called vestments. Some of the vestments that he wears are different colors for the different seasons of the Church year. The priest wears special clothing because he represents Jesus at Mass.

Crucifix

A crucifix is a cross with an image of Jesus on it. A crucifix is usually hung somewhere near the altar or is carried in procession as Mass begins.

Holy Water

As you enter the church, you dip your hand in holy water from the baptismal font or holy water font and make the Sign of the Cross. This reminds you of your Baptism.

Candles

Candles light the darkness. They are a sign of God's presence. Candles are carried during processions at Mass and are also placed on or beside the altar.

Paschal Candle

At Easter, the Paschal Candle is lit to remind the Church that Jesus is the light of the world. This candle is a very large candle from which many other baptismal candles are lit.

Vigil Lights

Some churches have special candles called vigil lights. They are usually blue, red, or amber. These candles are lit when people ask for special prayers.

The Four Parts of the Mass

1. The Introductory Rites

The Introductory Rites begin the Mass.

- A procession by the priest, deacon, and servers begins the Mass.
- The Church asks for God's mercy with the prayer: "Lord, have mercy. Christ, have mercy. Lord, have mercy."
- A song of glory and praise comes after that.

2. The Liturgy of the Word

The Liturgy of the Word is the first main part of the Mass.

- The community listens to a reading from the Old Testament and one from the New Testament.
- The priest or deacon reads the Gospel and gives a homily. During Mass Jesus is present. Christ is present in:
  - the assembled community.
  - the Word of God.
  - the presiding priest.
  - in his Body and Blood most especially.

3. The Liturgy of the Eucharist

The Liturgy of the Eucharist is the other great part of the Mass.

- Gifts of bread and wine are brought to the altar.
- The assembly remembers Jesus' Death and Resurrection.
- The Church offers praise and gives thanks to God through Jesus.
- Through the power of the Holy Spirit, and the words and actions of the priest, the bread and wine become the Body and Blood of Jesus.
- Before receiving Jesus in Holy Communion people offer one another a sign of peace by shaking hands or hugging.

4. The End of Mass

At the end of Mass, the priest blesses the people and tells them to go forth in peace to share about Jesus.

Catholics serve in the Mass in various ways: as altar servers, cross bearers, singers, readers, and extraordinary ministers of Holy Communion.

Liturgical Seasons and Colors

The Church has many seasons. Each season is marked by a special color or colors that decorate the church and the vestments that the priest wears.

Advent

Advent is the beginning of the Church year and is marked by the color violet. Advent is about four weeks long; it looks forward to the return of Jesus at the end of time, and it leads up to Christmas. It is a time of waiting and preparing.

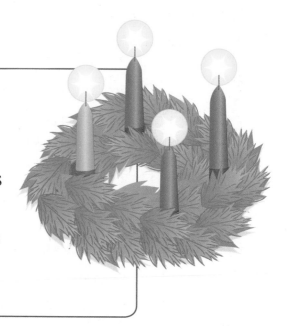

Christmas

Christmas is celebrated with the colors white and gold. Gold can be used instead of white for special Church holy days. At Christmas the Church remembers the birth of Jesus and celebrates his presence with us now. We look forward to the return of Jesus at the end of time.

Ordinary Time

Ordinary Time celebrates the words and works of Jesus and is marked by the color green.

Lent

During Lent Christians recall their baptismal promises to change their life and act more like Jesus. As a sign of preparation for Easter, Lent is marked by the color violet.

Easter Triduum

The Easter Triduum is the season that lasts for three days and is the most holy season of the Church year. It celebrates Jesus' passing through Death to life. The holy days of Triduum are Holy Thursday (white or gold), Good Friday (red), Holy Saturday (white or gold), and Easter Sunday (white or gold).

Easter

The Easter season starts on the night of Easter Sunday. Vestments are brilliant white for new life because the Easter season celebrates Jesus' Resurrection. Easter also celebrates the new life Jesus' Resurrection brings to all.

God's Laws

God knows it is sometimes difficult to make good choices. He gave his People the Ten Commandments to help guide them. He wants you to make good choices, too.

The Ten Commandments	What They Mean
1 I am the Lord your God: you shall not have strange gods before me.	Make God the most important thing in your life.
2 You shall not take the name of the Lord your God in vain.	Always use God's name in a reverent way.
3 Remember to keep holy the Lord's Day.	Attend Mass and rest on Sunday.
4 Honor your father and your mother.	Love and obey your parents and guardians.
5 You shall not kill.	Be kind to the people and animals God made; care for yourself and others.
6 You shall not commit adultery.	Be respectful of your body.
7 You shall not steal.	Don't take other people's things; don't take what belongs to someone else.
8 You shall not bear false witness against your neighbor.	Always tell the truth.
9 You shall not covet your neighbor's wife.	Keep your thoughts and words clean; don't be jealous of other people's friendships.
10 You shall not covet your neighbor's goods.	Be happy with the things you have; don't be jealous of what other people have.

Jesus' Command to Love

Jesus taught that the Great Commandment and his New Commandment sum up the Ten Commandments.

The Great Commandment

"You shall love the Lord, your God, with all your heart, with all your being, with all your strength, and with all your mind, and your neighbor as yourself." Luke 10:27

Jesus' New Commandment

"This is my commandment: love one another as I love you." John 15:12

Obeying God

God wants you to obey him. He asks you to love him and others with your whole heart. When you do this, your friendship with God grows stronger. When you choose to disobey God, you commit a sin.

Sin

A sin is a person's choice to disobey God on purpose and do something that he or she knows is wrong. When you sin, it hurts your friendship with God. You also hurt yourself and others when you do not choose to do good.

Accidents and Mistakes

When you make a mistake or have an accident you are not disobeying God. You do not choose to have an accident or make a mistake. Accidents and mistakes are not sins. You do not do them on purpose.

Forgiveness

God wants you to be close to him. When you sin, you can ask God for forgiveness and promise to make better choices. God forgives us when we are truly sorry and ask his forgiveness through the Church. God is always ready to forgive you. God's love for you never ends.

Gifts of the Holy Spirit

Through the Holy Spirit, God helps you grow in friendship with him and with others. You received the Gifts of the Holy Spirit at Baptism. These seven powerful gifts help you to follow the guidance of the Holy Spirit, and live as Jesus followers. They open your heart so that the Holy Spirit can guide you to make good and unselfish choices.

Gifts of the Holy Spirit

You receive the Gifts of the Holy Spirit through the Sacraments of Baptism and Confirmation. These gifts help you grow in relationship with God and others.

Wisdom
Understanding
Right Judgment (Counsel)
Courage (Fortitude)
Knowledge
Reverence (Piety)
Wonder and Awe (Fear of the Lord)

Basic Prayers

These are essential prayers that every Catholic should know. Latin is the official, universal language of the Church. No matter what language someone speaks in their daily life, these prayers are prayed in common in Latin.

Sign of the Cross

In the name of the Father,
and of the Son,
and of the Holy Spirit.
Amen.

Signum Crucis

In nómine Patris
et Fílii
et Spíritus Sancti.
Amen.

Glory Be

Glory be to the Father
and to the Son
and to the Holy Spirit,
as it was in the beginning
is now, and ever shall be
world without end. Amen.

Gloria Patri

Gloria Patri
et Fílio
et Spíritui Sancto.
Sicut erat in princípio,
et nunc et semper
et in sæ´cula sæculorem.
Amen.

The Lord's Prayer

Our Father,
who art in heaven,
hallowed be thy name;
thy kingdom come,
thy will be done
on earth as it is in heaven.
Give us this day our daily bread,
and forgive us our trespasses,
as we forgive those who trespass
against us;
and lead us not into temptation,
but deliver us from evil. Amen.

Pater Noster

Pater noster qui es in cælis:
santificétur Nomen Tuum;
advéniat Regnum Tuum;
fiat volúntas Tua,
sicut in cælo, et in terra.
Panem nostrum
cotidiánum da nobis hódie;
et dimítte nobis débita nostra,
sicut et nos
dimíttus debitóribus nostris;
et ne nos indúcas in
    tentatiónem;
sed líbera nos a Malo. Amen.

The Hail Mary

Hail, Mary, full of grace,
the Lord is with thee.
Blessed art thou among
    women
and blessed is the fruit of
    thy womb, Jesus.
Holy Mary, Mother of God,
pray for us sinners,
now and at the hour of
    our death. Amen.

Ave, Maria

Ave, María, grátia plena,
Dóminus tecum.
Benedícta tu in muliéribus,
et benedíctus fructus ventris
    tui, Iesus.
Sancta María, Mater Dei,
ora pro nobis peccatóribus,
nunc et in hora mortis nostræ.
Amen.

Personal and Family Prayers

Morning Prayer

Blessed are you, Lord, God of
all creation:
you take the sleep from my eyes
and the slumber from my
    eyelids.
Amen.

Evening Prayer

Protect us, Lord, as we stay
    awake;
watch over us as we sleep,
that awake, we may keep watch
    with Christ,
and asleep, rest in his peace.
Amen.

Grace After Meals

We give you thanks, Almighty
God, for all your gifts which
we have received through Christ
our Lord. Amen.

Act of Faith, Hope, and Love

*This prayer is often prayed in the
morning to remind us that all gifts come
from God, and that he can help us
believe, trust, and love.*

My God, I believe in you,
    I hope in you,
I love you above all things,
    with all my mind
and heart and strength.

Grace Before Meals

Bless us, O Lord, and these
    thy gifts
which we are about to receive
from thy bounty, through
Christ our Lord. Amen.

Angel Guardian (traditional)

An angel is a spiritual being that is messenger of God. Angels are mentioned nearly 300 times in the Bible. Three important angels are Gabriel, Michael, and Raphael.

Angel of God,
my guardian dear,
to whom his love commits me here.
Ever this day,
be at my side,
to light and guard,
to rule and guide. Amen.

Angel Guardian (contemporary)

Angel sent by God to guide me,
be my light and walk beside me;
be my guardian and protect me;
on the paths of life direct me.

Praying with the Saints

When we pray with the Saints, we ask them to pray to God for us and to pray with us. The Saints are with Christ. They speak for us when we need help.

A litany is a prayer with one line that is meant to be repeated over and over again so that those praying are caught up in the prayer itself. Some litanies are to Jesus; others are known as Litanies of the Saints, on whom we call to intercede for us.

Litanies

Lord, have mercy.
Lord, have mercy.
Christ, have mercy.
Christ, have mercy.
Lord, have mercy.
Lord, have mercy.

Holy Mary, Mother of God,
   pray for us
Saint John the Baptist,
   pray for us
Saint Joseph, pray for us
Saint Peter and Saint Paul,
   pray for us

Lord [Jesus], we ask you,
   hear our prayer.
Lord [Jesus], we ask you,
   hear our prayer.

Christ, hear us.
Christ, graciously hear us.

Prayer of Petition

Lord God, you know our
   weakness.
In your mercy grant that the
   example of your Saints may
   bring us back to love and
   serve you through Christ
   our Lord.
Amen.

Catholic **Faith Words**

A

angel a type of spiritual being that does God's work, such as delivering messages from God or helping to keep people safe from harm **(211)**

B

Baptism the Sacrament in which a person is immersed in water or has water poured on him or her. Baptism takes away Original Sin and all personal sin, and makes a person a child of God and member of the Church. **(291)**

Bible the Word of God written in human words. The Bible is the holy book of the Church. **(67)**

C

Church the community of all baptized people who believe in God and follow Jesus **(189)**

Commandment a law that God made for people to obey **(161)**

creation everything made by God **(67)**

D

disciple a follower of Jesus who believes in him and lives by his teachings **(228)**

E

Eucharist the Sacrament in which Jesus shares himself, and the bread and wine become his Body and Blood **(307)**

F

faith believing in God and all that he helps us understand about himself. Faith leads us to obey God. **(148)**

free will being able to choose whether to obey God or disobey God. God created us with free will because he wants us to make good choices. **(240)**

G

God the Father the First Divine Person of the Holy Trinity **(108)**

godparents two people chosen by your parents to help you follow Jesus. They are usually present at your Baptism. **(293)**

grace God's gift of a share in his life and help **(291)**

Great Commandment the law to love God above all else and to love others the way you love yourself **(161)**

Heaven the full joy of living with God forever (318)

holy unique and pure; set apart for God and his purposes (211)

Holy Communion receiving Jesus' Body and Blood in the celebration of the Eucharist (308)

Holy Family the name for the human family of Jesus, Mary, and Joseph (120)

Holy Spirit the Third Divine Person of the Holy Trinity (198)

Holy Trinity the one God in three Divine Persons—God the Father, God the Son, and God the Holy Spirit (109)

image of God the likeness of God that is in all human beings because we are created by him (90)

Jesus the name of the Son of God who became man (78)

Kingdom of God the world of love, peace, and justice that is in Heaven and is still being built on Earth (189)

Last Supper the meal Jesus shared with his disciples the night before he died. At the Last Supper, Jesus gave himself in the Eucharist. (307)

Lord's Prayer the prayer Jesus taught his followers to pray to God the Father. This prayer is also called the Our Father. (173)

Mary the Mother of Jesus, the Mother of God. She is also called "Our Lady" because she is our Mother and the Mother of the Church. (120)

Mass the gathering of Catholics to worship God. It includes readings from the Bible and the celebration of Holy Communion. (308)

New Testament the second part of the Bible about the life and teachings of Jesus, his followers, and the early Church (133)

obey to do things or act in certain ways that are requested by those in authority (240)

Old Testament the first part of the Bible about God and his People before Jesus was born (133)

Original Sin the first sin committed by Adam and Eve and passed down to everyone **(266)**

peace when things are calm and people get along with one another **(332)**

praise giving God honor and thanks because he is God **(78)**

prayer talking to and listening to God **(170)**

Resurrection the event of Jesus being raised from Death to new life by God the Father through the power of the Holy Spirit **(269)**

Saint a hero of the Church who loved God very much, led a holy life, and is now with God in Heaven **(211)**

serve to help or give others what they need in a loving way **(226)**

Seven Sacraments special signs and celebrations that Jesus gave his Church. The Sacraments allow us to share in the life and work of God. **(279)**

sin a person's choice to disobey God on purpose and do what he or she knows is wrong. Accidents and mistakes are not sins. **(251)**

Son of God a name for Jesus that tells you God is his Father. The Son of God is the Second Divine Person of the Holy Trinity. **(108)**

Ten Commandments God's laws that tell people how to love him and others **(239)**

thanksgiving giving thanks to God for all he has given us **(81)**

Index

Index